LETTERS OF NOTE: SEX

Letters of Note was born in 2009 with the launch of lettersofnote.com, a website celebrating old-fashioned correspondence that has since been visited over 100 million times. The first *Letters of Note* volume was published in October 2013, followed later that year by the first Letters Live, an event at which world-class performers delivered remarkable letters to a live audience.

Since then, these two siblings have grown side by side, with *Letters of Note* becoming an international phenomenon, and Letters Live shows being staged at iconic venues around the world, from London's Royal Albert Hall to the theatre at the Ace Hotel in Los Angeles.

You can find out more at lettersofnote.com and letterslive.com. And now you can also listen to the audio editions of the new series of *Letters of Note*, read by an extraordinary cast drawn from the wealth of talent that regularly takes part in the acclaimed Letters Live shows.

Letters of Note

COMPILED BY

Shaun Usher

PENGUIN BOOKS

For Play

PENGUIN BOOKS
An imprint of Penguin Random House LLC
penguinrandomhouse.com

First published in Great Britain by Canongate Books Ltd 2021
Published in Penguin Books 2021

LIBRARY OF CONGRESS CATALOGING-IN-PUBLICATION DATA
Names: Usher, Shaun, 1978– compiler.
Title: Letters of note. Sex / compiled by Shaun Usher.
Description: New York : Penguin Books, 2021. |
Series: Letters of note.
Identifiers: LCCN 2021022655 (print) | LCCN 2021022656 (ebook) |
ISBN 9780143134718 (paperback) | ISBN 9780525506522 (ebook)
Subjects: LCSH: Sex—Social aspects. | Letters.
Classification: LCC HQ16 .L56 2021 (print) |
LCC HQ16 (ebook) | DDC 306.7—dc23
LC record available at https://lccn.loc.gov/2021022655
LC ebook record available at https://lccn.loc.gov/2021022656

Printed in the United States of America
1st Printing

Set in Joanna MT

CONTENTS

A letter is a time bomb, a message in a bottle, a spell, a cry for help, a story, an expression of concern, a ladle of love, a way to connect through words. This simple and brilliantly democratic art form remains a potent means of communication and, regardless of whatever technological revolution we are in the middle of, the letter lives and, like literature, it always will.

INTRODUCTION

Before I begin: should you happen to be a child, please close this book and hand it to an adult. If you are an adult, please do not leave this book within reach of a child, no matter how keen a letter writer they might be. Instead, may I suggest introducing them to some of the more age-appropriate titles in this series, beginning with *Letters of Note: Dogs* and *Letters of Note: Cats*.

Letters of Note: Sex, should you be in any doubt, is a book about sex. More specifically, it is an exploration of sex, and our relationship to it, through the lens of the humble letter – a form of correspondence which, given its ostensibly private nature, is perfectly suited to discussing such intimate matters.

Both tone and focus of these letters are wide-ranging. We begin with a letter of sisterly advice from anthropologist Margaret Mead to her younger sibling who had recently had her first sexual experience; we end, 150 pages later, with a missive from Australian composer Percy Grainger that is so sexually explicit as to approach the surreal. The journey from first to last is winding.

You will read a pained plea from the founder of
the Catholic Worker Movement to the man with
whom she longed to share her bed but for reasons
of religion could not; you will see the request once
sent to a member of the Rolling Stones by a sculptor
who wished to immortalise his 'spectacular'
instrument; and you will, I hope, be fascinated by a
frank exchange of letters between two novelists
in which is discussed the 'last sexual taboo.' Topics
broached in these unabashed pages include
masturbation, prostitution, celibacy, promiscuity,
incest, sex toys, pornography, BDSM, bestiality,
erectile dysfunction, and pubic lice, and they come
through the pens and typewriters of such people
as Anaïs Nin, Frida Kahlo, Martha Gellhorn,
Mae West, Marcel Proust, Henry Miller, Dian
Fossey, and Georgia O'Keeffe. A heady mix indeed.

Since work on this volume began in 2019 I have
trawled through thousands of letters, flicked
through hundreds of books, and entered millions
of alarm-triggering words and phrases into search
engines, all in search of the selection you now
hold, and I am of the firm opinion that each one
deserves its place. I hope you will agree.

Shaun Usher
2020

The Letters

LETTER 01
AN INSTRUMENT OF JOY
Margaret Mead to Elizabeth Mead
11 January 1926

Margaret Mead was widely regarded as the leading anthropologist in the western world for many years, thanks largely to Coming of Age in Samoa, a ground-breaking and controversial book she wrote after a research trip in 1925. In the book, she sought to shine a light on the previously alien lives and relaxed sexual attitudes of adolescent Samoan girls. Although since contested, Mead's findings were a revelation at the time and in fact have been credited with influencing the sexual revolution of the 1960s. In 1926, a year after setting foot on the Samoan island of Ta'ū, Mead learnt of a sexual awakening much closer to home: that of her younger sister, Elizabeth. This letter of advice was her response.

THE LETTER

Elizabeth dear, I've a good mind to punish you by writing back in pencil. You're a wretch to write in pencil on pink paper just when you're writing something very important that you particularly want me to read. Don't do it again.

I am glad you told me about the moonlight party, dear. It's the sort of thing that had to happen sometime and it might have been a great deal worse. As it was, it was a nice boy whom you like, and nothing that need worry you. There are two things I'd like to have you remember—or in fact several. The thrills you get from touching the body of another person are just as good and legitimate thrills as those you get at the opera. Only the ones which [you] get at the opera are all mixed up with your ideas of beauty and music and Life—and so they seem to you good and holy things. In the same way the best can only be had from the joys which life offers to our sense of touch (for sex is mostly a matter of the sense of touch) when we associate those joys with love and respect and understanding.

All the real tragedies of sex come from disassociation—either of the old maid who sternly refuses to think about sex at all until finally she can think about nothing else—and goes crazy—or of the man who goes from one wanton's arms to another seeking only the immediate sensation of the moment and never linking it up with other parts of his life. It is by the way in which sex—and under this I include warm demonstrative friendships with both sexes as well as love affairs proper with men—is linked with all the other parts of our lives, with our appreciation of music and our tenderness for little children, and most of all with our love for someone and the additional nearness to them which expression of love gives us, that sex itself is given meaning.

You must realize that your body has been given you as an instrument of joy—and tho you should choose most rigorously whose touch may make that instrument thrill and sing a thousand beautiful songs—you must never think it wrong of it to sing. For your body was made to sing to another's touch and the flesh itself is not wise to choose. It is the spirit within the body which must be stern and say—"No, you can not play on this my precious instrument. True it would sing for you. Your fingers are very clever at playing on such instruments—but I do not love you, nor respect you—and I will not have my body singing a tune which my soul cannot sing also." If you remember this, you will never be filled with disgust of any sort. Any touch may set the delicate chords humming—but it is your right to choose who shall really play a tune—and be very very sure of your choices first. To have given a kiss where only a handshake was justified by the love behind it—*that* is likely to leave a bad taste in your mouth.

And for the other part—about being boy crazy. Try to think of boys as people, some nice, some indifferent—not as a class. You are[n't] *girl* crazy are you? Then why should you be *boy* crazy? If a boy is [an] interesting *person*, why, like him. If he isn't, don't. Think of him as an individual first and as a boy second. What kind of a person he is is a great deal more important than that he belongs to the other sex—after all so do some hundred million other individuals.

I am very proud of the way you are able to think thru the problems which life brings you—and of the way you meet them. And I consider it a great privilege to have you tell me about them. I'm so glad you are happy dear.

Very lovingly,
Margaret

LETTER 02
WHAT GLOOMY TIDINGS ABOUT THE CRABS

Patrick Leigh Fermor to Enrica Huston
11 August 1961

Patrick Leigh Fermor was a dashing English war hero and journalist who produced some of the most celebrated travel writing of modern times, not least in A Time of Gifts, a compelling account of a year-long trek from Rotterdam to the ancient city of Constantinople. The journey took place in 1934, forty-three years before the book's eventual publication. Fermor's charms and propensity to party were well known, resulting in affairs with various women in numerous countries over the years, including, in the 1960s, ballerina Enrica 'Ricki' Huston, who happened to be married to Hollywood filmmaker John Huston. It was to her that Fermor wrote in August of 1961, in relation to a mutual infestation they were both itching to get to the bottom of.

THE LETTER

The Mill House
Dumbleton

My darling Ricki,

1,000 thanks for your Paris letter, and apologies for delay. Barbara and Niko came for the weekend, and I had to go to London when they left, with the result that now – Tuesday evening! – just back, I can only get this off express to Paris tomorrow morning. Damn, damn, damn.

Triple damn indeed, and sixfold & 100-fold because alas! I've committed myself, only yesterday too, to devoting myself to my *mama* in the country this weekend, and I'm such a neglectful and intermittent son that I can't put it off now. [. . .] I am longing to see you and hate the thought of your vanishing out of reach for what seems such an age, all unembraced! Bugger (cubed).

I say, what gloomy tidings about the CRABS! *Could* it be me? I'll tell you why this odd doubt exists: [. . .] just after arriving back in London from Athens, I was suddenly alerted by what *felt* like the beginnings of troop-movements in the fork, but on scrutiny, expecting an aerial view of general mobilisation, there was nothing to be seen, not even a scout, a spy, or a despatch rider. Puzzled, I watched and waited and soon even the preliminary tramplings died away, so I assumed, as the happy summer days of peace followed each other, that the incident, or the delusive shudder through the chancelleries, was over. While this faint scare was on, knowing that, thanks to lunar tyranny, it couldn't be from you, I assumed (and please spare my blushes here!) that the handover bid must have occurred by dint of a meeting with an old pal in Paris, which, I'm sorry to announce, ended in brief carnal knowledge, more for *auld lang syne* than any more pressing reason. On getting your letter, I made a dash for privacy and thrashed through the undergrowth, but found everything almost eerily calm: fragrant and silent glades that might never have known the invader's tread. The whole thing makes me scratch my head, if I may so put it. But I bet your trouble *does* come from me, because the crabs of the world seem to fly to me, like the children of Israel to Abraham's bosom, a sort of ambulant Canaan. I've been a real martyr to them. What must have happened is this. A tiny, picked, cunning, and well-camouflaged commando must have landed while I was in Paris and then *lain up*, seeing me merely as a stepping stone or a spring-board to better things, and, when you came within striking distance, knowing the highest when they saw it, they struck (as who wouldn't?) and then deployed in force, leaving their first beachhead empty. Or so I think! (Security will be tightened up. They may have left an agent with a radio who is playing a waiting game . . .)

I wonder whether I have reconstructed the facts all right. I do hope so; I couldn't bear it to be anyone but me. But at the same time, if it is me, v. v. many apologies. There's some wonderful Italian powder you can get in France called MOM — another indication of a matriarchal society — which is worth its weight in gold dust. It is rather sad to think that their revels now are ended, that the happy woods (where I would fain be, wandering in pensive mood) where they held high holiday will soon be a silent grove. Where are all their quips and quiddities? The pattering of tiny feet will be stilled. Bare, ruin'd choirs. Don't tell anyone about this private fauna. Mom's the word, gentle reader. [. . .]

No more now, my darling Ricki, as I must leap into my faithful Standard Companion and dash to the post with this, hoping and praying it gets you in time. No need to say how much I'm going to miss you; you know I will. Not only the moon's a rival now, but the sun and Greece as well, and I

know what potent allies they are. But no moping!
We'll make some glowing plan when you get back,
and.see what magic the mysterious north can offer.
Anyway, bless you a billion times, my dearest
darling Ricki, and lots of love hugs and kisses

from Paddy

LETTER 03
YOU THE PIOUS, THE MORAL, THE RESPECTABLE

Another Unfortunate to *The Times*
February 1858

On 25 February 1858, Charles Dickens wrote to the editor of The Times *and enquired as to the true identity of a sex worker who had recently written to the paper under the pseudonym 'Another Unfortunate'. Dickens was writing in his capacity as co-founder of Urania Cottage, a home for 'fallen women' who had 'turned to a life of immorality', and his hope, by writing, was to contact and save another. Alas, it was not to be. The next day, having belatedly read Another Unfortunate's letter in full – reprinted here – and now keenly aware that this particular lady most certainly did not wish to be rescued, Dickens wrote to the editor again and withdrew his request. In reality, Another Unfortunate had in fact been responding to an earlier letter in* The Times *from 'One More Unfortunate' supposedly by an ashamed sex worker who believed that women like her 'are beings whom men should shun and women should condemn'.*

THE LETTER

Sir – another 'Unfortunate', but of a class entirely different from the one who has already instructed the public in your columns, presumes to address you.

I am a stranger to all the fine sentiments which still linger in the bosom of your correspondent. I have none of those youthful recollections which, contrasting her early days with her present life, aggravate the misery of the latter. My parents did not give me any education; they did not instil into my mind virtuous precepts nor set me a good example. All my experiences in early life were gleaned among associates who knew nothing of the laws of God but by dim tradition and faint report, and whose chiefest triumphs of wisdom consisted in picking their way through the paths of destitution in which they were cast by cunning evasion or in open defiance of the laws of man.

I do not think of my parents (long in their graves) with any such compunctions as your correspondent describes. They gave me in their lifetime, according to their means and knowledge, and as they had probably received from their parents, shelter and protection, mixed with curses and caresses. I received all as a matter of course, and, knowing nothing better, was content in that kind of contentedness which springs from insensibility; I returned their affection in like kind as they gave it to me. As long as they lived, I looked up to them as my parents. I assisted them in their poverty, and made them comfortable. They looked on me and I on them with pride, for I was proud to be able to minister to their wants; and as for shame, although they knew perfectly well the means by which I obtained money, I do assure you, Sir, that by them, as by myself, my success was regarded as the reward of a proper ambition, and was a source of real pleasure and gratification.

Let me tell you something of my parents. My father's most profitable occupation was brick-making. When not employed at this, he did anything he could get to do. My mother worked with him in the brickfield, and so did I and a progeny of brothers and sisters; for somehow or other, although my parents occupied a very unimportant space in the world, it pleased God to make them fruitful. We all slept in the same room. There were few privacies, few family secrets in our house.

Father and mother both loved drink. In the household expenses, had accounts been kept, gin or beer would have been the heaviest items. We, the children, were indulged occasionally with a drop, but my honoured parents reserved to themselves the exclusive privilege of getting drunk, 'and they were the same as their parents had been'. I give you a chapter of the history of common life which may be stereotyped as the history of generation upon generation.

We knew not anything of religion. Sometimes when a neighbour died we went to the burial, and thus got within a few steps of the church. If a grand funeral chanced to fall in our way we went to see that, too—the fine black horses and nodding plumes—as we went to see the soldiers when we could for a lark. No parson ever came near us. The place where we lived was too dirty for nicely-shod gentlemen. 'The Publicans and Sinners' of our circumscribed, but thickly populated locality had no 'friend' among them.

Our neighbourhood furnished many subjects to the treadmill, the hulks, and the colonies, and some to the gallows. We lived with the fear of those things, and not with the fear of God before our eyes.

I was a very pretty child, and had a sweet voice; of course I used to sing. Most London boys and girls of the lower classes sing. 'My face is my fortune, kind sir, she said', was the ditty on which I bestowed most pains, and my father and mother would wink knowingly as I sang it. The latter would also tell me how pretty she was when young, and how she sang, and what a fool she had been, and how well she might have done had she been wise.

Frequently we had quite a stir in our colony. Some young lady who had quitted the paternal restraints, or perhaps, had started off, none knew whither or how, to seek her fortune, would reappear among us with a profusion of ribands, fine clothes, and lots of cash. Visiting the neighbours, treating indiscriminately, was the order of the day on such occasions, without any more definite information of the means by which the dazzling transformation had been effected than could be conveyed by knowing winks and the words 'luck' and 'friends'. Then she would disappear and leave us in our dirt, penury, and obscurity. You cannot conceive, Sir, how our ambition was stirred by these visitations.

Now commences an important era in my life. I was a fine, robust, healthy girl, 13 years of age. I had larked with the boys of my own age. I had huddled with them, boys and girls together, all night long in our common haunts. I had seen much and heard abundantly of the mysteries of the sexes. To me such things had been matters of common sight and common talk. For some time I had coquetted on the verge of a strong curiosity, and a natural desire, and without a particle of affection, scarce a partiality, I lost—what? not my virtue, for I never had any. That which is commonly, but untruly called virtue, I gave away.

You reverend Mr Philanthropist—what call you virtue? Is it not the principle, the essence, which keeps watch and ward over the conduct, the substance, the materiality? No such principle ever kept watch and ward over me, and I repeat that I never lost that which I never had – my virtue.

According to my own ideas at the time I only extended my rightful enjoyments. Opportunity was not long wanting to put my newly acquired knowledge to profitable use. In the commencement of my fifteenth year one of our be-ribanded visitors took me off, and introduced me to the great world, and thus commenced my career as what you better classes call a prostitute. I cannot say that I felt any other shame than the bashfulness of a noviciate introduced to strange society. Remarkable for good looks, and no less so for good temper, I gained money, dressed gaily, and soon agreeably astonished my parents and old neighbours by making a descent upon them.

Passing over the vicissitudes of my course, alternating between reckless gaiety and extreme destitution, I improved myself greatly; and at the age of 15 was living partly under the protection of one who thought he discovered that I had talent, and some good qualities as well as beauty, who treated me more kindly and considerately than I had ever before been treated, and thus drew from me something like a feeling of regard, but not sufficiently strong to lift me to that sense of my position which the so-called virtuous and respectable members of society seem to entertain. Under the protection of this gentleman, and encouraged by him, I commenced the work of my education; that portion of education which is comprised in some knowledge of my own language and the ordinary accomplishments of my sex; – moral science, as I believe it is called, has always been an enigma to me, and is so to this day. I suppose it is because I am one of those who, as Rousseau says, are 'born to be prostitutes'. Common honesty I believe in rigidly. I have always paid my debts, and, though I say it, I have always been charitable to my fellow creatures. I have not neglected my duty to my family. I supported my parents while they lived, and buried them decently when they died. I paid a celebrated lawyer heavily

for defending unsuccessfully my eldest brother,
who had the folly to be caught in the commission
of a robbery. I forgave him the offence against the
law in the theft, and the offence against discretion
in being caught. This cost me some effort, for I
always abhorred stealing. I apprenticed my younger
brother to a good trade, and helped him into a
little business. Drink frustrated my efforts in his
behalf. Through the influence of a very influential
gentleman, a very particular friend of mine, he is
now a well-conducted member of the police. My
sisters, whose early life was in all respects the
counterpart of my own, I brought out and started
in the world. The elder of the two is kept by a
nobleman, the next by an officer in the army; the
third has not yet come to years of discretion, and
is 'having her fling' before she settles down.

Now, what if I am a prostitute, what business
has society to abuse me? Have I received any
favours at the hands of society? If I am a hideous
cancer in society, are not the causes of the disease
to be sought in the rottenness of the carcass? Am I
not its legitimate child; no bastard, Sir? Why does
my unnatural parent repudiate me, and what has
society ever done for me, that I should do anything
for it, and what have I ever done against society
that it should drive me into a corner and crush me

to the earth? I have neither stolen (at least since I was a child), nor murdered, nor defrauded. I earn my money and pay my way, and try to do good with it, according to my ideas of good. I do not get drunk, nor fight, nor create uproar in the streets or out of them. I do not use bad language. I do not offend the public eye by open indecencies. I go to the Opera, I go to Almack's, I go to the theatres, I go to quiet, well-conducted casinos, I go to all the places of public amusement, behaving myself with as much propriety as society can exact. I pay business visits to my tradespeople, the most fashionable of the West-end. My milliners, my silkmercers, my bootmakers, know, all of them, who I am and how I live, and they solicit my patronage as earnestly and cringingly as if I were Madam, the Lady of the right rev, patron of the Society for the Suppression of Vice. They find my money as good and my pay better (for we are robbed on every hand) than that of Madam, my Lady; and, if all the circumstances and conditions of our lives had been reversed, would Madam, my Lady, have done better or been better than I?

I speak of others as well as for myself, for the very great majority, nearly all the real undisguised prostitutes in London, spring from my class, and are made by and under pretty much such conditions of life as I have narrated, and particularly by untutored and unrestrained intercourse of the sexes in early life. We come from the dregs of society, as our so-called betters term it. What business has society to have dregs—such dregs as we? You railers of the Society for the Suppression of Vice, you the pious, the moral, the respectable, as you call yourselves, who stand on your smooth and pleasant side of the great gulf you have dug and keep between yourselves and the dregs, why don't you bridge it over, or fill it up, and by some humane and generous process absorb us into your leavened mass, until we become interpenetrated with goodness like yourselves? [. . .]

What have we to be ashamed of, we who do not know what shame is—the shame you mean? I conduct myself prudently, and defy you and your policemen too. Why stand you there mouthing with sleek face about morality? What is morality? Will you make us responsible for what we never knew? Teach us what is right and tutor us in what is good before you punish us for doing wrong. We who are the real prostitutes of the true natural growth of society, and no impostors, will not be judged by 'One more unfortunate', nor measured by any standard of her setting up. She is a mere chance intruder in our ranks, and has no business there. She does understand what shame means and knows all about it, at least so it seems, and if she has a particle left, let her accept 'Amicus's' kind offer as soon as possible.

Like 'One more unfortunate' there are other intruders among us—a few, very few, 'victims of seduction'. But [seduction] is not the root of the evil—scarcely a fibre of the root. A rigorous law should be passed and rigorously carried out to punish seduction, but it will not perceptibly thin the ranks of prostitution. Seduction is the common story of numbers of well brought up, who never were seduced, and who are voluntary and inexcusable profligates. Vanity and idleness send us a large body of recruits. Servant girls, who wish to ape their mistress' finery, and whose wages won't permit them to do so honestly—these set up seduction as their excuse. Married women, who have no respect for their husbands, and are not content with their lawful earnings, these are the worst among us, and it is a pity they cannot be picked out and punished. They have no principle of any kind and are a disgrace to us. If I were a married woman I would be true to my husband. I speak for my class, the regular standing army of the force.

Gentlemen of philanthropic societies and members of the Society for the Suppression of Vice may build reformatories and open houses of refuge and Magdalen asylums, and 'Amicus' may save occasionally a 'fallen sister' who can prevail on herself to be saved; but we who never were sisters—who never had any relationship, part, interest, or communion with the large family of this world's virtues, moralities, and proprieties—we, who are not fallen, but were always down—who never had any virtue to lose—we who are the natural growth of things, and are constantly ripening for the harvest—who, interspersed in our little, but swarming colonies throughout the kingdom at large, hold the source of supply and keep it fruitful—what do they propose to do with us? Cannot society devise some plan to reach us?

'One more unfortunate' proposes a 'skimming' progress. But what of the great bubbling cauldron? Remove from the streets a score or two of 'foreign women', and 'double as many English', and you diminish the competition of those that remain; the quiet, clever, cunning cajolers described by 'One more unfortunate'. You hide a prurient pimple of the 'great sin' with a patch of that plaster known as the 'observance of propriety', and nothing more. You 'miss' the evil, but it is existent still. After all it is something to save the eye from offence, so remove them; and not only a score or two, but something like two hundred foreign women, whose open and disgusting indecencies and practices have contributed more than anything else to bring on our heads the present storm of indignation. It is rare that English women, even prostitutes, give cause of gross public offence. Cannot they be packed off to their own countries with their base, filthy and filthy-living men, whom they maintain, and clothe, and feed, to superintend their fortunes, and who are a still greater disgrace to London than these women are?

Hurling big figures at us, it is said that there are 80,000 of us in London alone—which is a monstrous falsehood—and of those 80,000, poor hardworking sewing girls, sewing women, are numbered in by thousands, and called indiscriminately prostitutes; writing, preaching, speechifying, that they have lost their virtue too.

It is a cruel calumny to call them in mass prostitutes; and, as for their virtue, they lose it as one loses his watch who is robbed by the highway thief. Their virtue is the watch, and society is the thief. These poor women toiling on starvation wages, while penury, misery, and famine clutch them by the throat and say, 'Render up your body or die'.

Admire this magnificent shop in this fashionable street; its front, fittings, and decorations cost no less than a thousand pounds. The respectable master of the establishment keeps his carriage and lives in his country-house. He has daughters too; his patronesses are fine ladies, the choicest impersonations of society. Do they think, as they admire the taste and elegance of that tradesman's show, of the poor creatures who wrought it, and what they were paid for it? Do they reflect on the weary toiling fingers, on the eyes dim with watching, on the bowels yearning with hunger, on the bended frames, on the broken constitutions, on poor human nature driven to its coldest corner and reduced to its narrowest means in the production of these luxuries and adornments? This is an old story! Would it not be truer and more charitable to call these poor souls 'victims'?—some gentler, some more humane name than prostitute—to soften by some Christian expression if you cannot better the un-Christian system, the opprobrium of a fate to which society has driven them by the direst straits? What business has society to point its finger in scorn, to raise its voice in reprobation of them? Are they not its children, born of the cold indifference, of its callous selfishness, of its cruel pride?

Sir, I have trespassed on your patience beyond limit, and yet much remains to be said [. . . The difficulty of dealing with the evil is not so great as society considers it. Setting aside 'the sin', we are not so bad as we are thought to be. The difficulty is for society to set itself, with the necessary earnestness, self-humiliation, and self-denial, to the work. To deprive us of proper and harmless amusements, to subject us in mass to the pressure of force—of force wielded, for the most part, by ignorant, and often by brutal men—is only to add the cruelty of active persecution to the cruelty of passive indifference which made us as we are.

I remain, your humble servant,
Another Unfortunate.

LETTER 04
TO MY EVER-LOVING WIFE
Don to his wife
1 April 1968

On 1 April 1968, a British gentleman named Don fed a sheet of London Borough of Hounslow stationery into a typewriter and wrote a letter to his wife.

THE LETTER

LONDON BOROUGH OF HOUNSLOW

1st April, 1968

To my ever-loving wife,
During the past year I have attempted to seduce
you 365 times. I succeeded 36 times.

This averages once every 10 days and the
following is the list of reasons why I did not
succeed:

We will wake your mother: 7 times
It is too hot: 15 times
It is too cold: 3 times
Too tired: 19 times
Too late: 16 times
Too early: 9 times
Pretending to sleep: 35 times
Window open, neighbours will hear: 3 times
Backache: 16 times
Toothache: 2 times
Headache: 6 times
Not in the mood: 21 times
Will make the cat jealous: 18 times
Watched late show: 12 times
Mud-pack: 3 times

Grease on face: 4 times

Too drunk: 17 times

Company in the next room: 7 times

Mind my hair: 28 times

Is that all you think about? 83 times

Do you think we can improve on our record this coming year?

Your ever-loving husband,

Don

'DO YOU THINK WE
CAN IMPROVE ON
OUR RECORD THIS
COMING YEAR?'

— Don

LETTER 05
THE ACHE IN MY HEART IS INTOLERABLE
Dorothy Day to Forster Batterham
10 December 1932

In 1924, journalist and social activist Dorothy Day met and fell in love with Forster Batterham, a biologist and anarchist with whom she would have a daughter, Tamar, in 1926. It was around the time of their child's birth that Day's religious beliefs deepened, leading to her conversion to Catholicism the next year. With Batterham fundamentally opposed to the concept of marriage due to his adherence to anarchism, they saw no option but for him to leave, resulting in many years of sexual longing and frustration as they lived apart. This letter was written in 1932 and marked the death of their ever-dwindling romance. It was sent shortly before Day founded the Catholic Worker Movement.

THE LETTER

Dear Forster—

I got your letter Friday afternoon and I've been pondering since whether or not to answer it. It doesn't seem much use, but still I can't let some of your statements go without telling you what I feel.

As to my feeling about sex, I do indeed now feel that sex is taboo outside of marriage. The institution of marriage has been built up by society as well as the Church to safeguard the home and children as well as people who don't know how to take care of themselves. Of course anyone who is sane and sound mentally will agree that promiscuity and looseness in sex is an ugly and inharmonious thing. You have always in the past treated me most casually, and I see no special difference between our affair and any other casual affair I have had in the past. You avoided, as you admitted yourself, all responsibility. You would not marry me then because you preferred the slight casual contact with me to any other. And last spring when my love and physical desire for you overcame me, you were quite willing for the affair to go on, on a weekend basis.

31

Sex is not at all taboo with me except outside of marriage. I am as free and unsuppressed as I ever was about it. I think the human body a beautiful thing, and the joys that a healthy body have are perfectly legitimate joys. I see no immediate difference between enjoying sex and enjoying a symphony concert, but sex having such a part in life, as producing children, has been restricted as society and the Church have felt best for the children.

I believe that in breaking these laws one is letting the flesh get an upper hand over the spirit, so I do not want to break these laws.

St. Augustine says, "If bodies please thee, praise God on occasion of them." And I feel no sorrow for all the joys we have had in the past together.

When I laughingly spoke about many a young girl holding out—you should have understood what I meant. You seem to think that one should always succumb immediately to any promptings of the flesh, and you think of it as unnatural and unhealthy to restrain oneself on account of the promptings of the spirit. What I meant was that many people in the past have observed the conventions and rules, for the sake not only of convention but of principle. It is hard for me to talk to you seriously,—you despise so utterly the things which mean so much to me. I wish you'd read more of Aldous Huxley, and imbibe a little of his rational tolerance.

You think all this is only hard on you. But I am suffering too. The ache in my heart is intolerable at times, and sometimes for days I can feel your lips upon me, waking and sleeping. It is because I love you so much that I want you to marry me. I want to be in your arms every night, as I used to be, and be with you always. I always loved you more than you did me. That is why I made up with you so many times, and went after you after we had had some quarrel. We always differed on principle, and now that I am getting older I cannot any longer always give way to you just because flesh has such power over me.

Of course I understand your allusion to smoking and drinking and such indulgences, and as I said before, I do agree with you and would give them all up for you. I really don't think I over-indulge very often. I consider drink only sinful inasmuch as it affects one's health, and I'm most ashamed for every time I do over-indulge. Sex and eating and drinking may easily be put in the same class since they are both physical gratifications. Still, even the slightest sexual lapse may have terrible and far-reaching consequences and so these laws have been built up. Of course all intelligent people can say—Oh, I'm so smart this doesn't apply to me, but I think that such laws, whether one considers them human or divine, have to be obeyed by all. It all is hopeless of course, tho it has often seemed to me a simple thing. Imaginatively I can understand your hatred and rebellion against my beliefs and I can't blame you. I have really given up hope now, so I won't try to persuade you any more.

Dorothy

LETTER 06
ALL I KNOW IS ASTHMA
Marcel Proust to Jacques Porel
July 1919

It is fair to say 1919 began badly for Marcel Proust, the influential French writer responsible for the classic multi-volume novel In Search of Lost Time. *Bedbound with laryngitis and seriously asthmatic, Proust received the unwelcome news that the building in Paris in which he had been living for more than a decade had been sold, leaving him with just a few months to find a new home and move his belongings. In May he accepted an offer from his good friend Jacques Porel to relocate to Rue Laurent-Pichat and settle for a few months in the same building as Porel's mother, the famous actress known simply as Réjane. Much to Proust's dismay, the walls were paper-thin and the noises were loud. By October, he had moved on.*

THE LETTER

My dear Jacques,

I shall have left the rue Laurent-Pichat by the time you get back. I'll miss the black-and-white flowers on the red background. But I've written a description of them which I'll send you as soon as I've moved. [. . .]

Kindly inform your Mother that I keep neither piano nor mistress at rue Laurent-Pichat. I'm not to blame for the noises that bring complaints from every floor in turn. Whereas my neighbours on the other side of the partition make love with a frenzy which makes me jealous. When I think that this sensation has less effect on me than a glass of cold beer, I envy people who are capable of uttering such cries that, at first, I thought someone was being murdered, but I realized what was happening when the woman's cries quickly resumed an octave below the man's, and was reassured. This racket, which must be audible over distances as great as the cry of those mating whales described by Michelet as rising like the twin towers of Notre Dame, is no fault of mine. All I know is asthma [. . .]

No sooner is the last cry achieved than they rush off to take a Sitz bath, their murmurs fading into the sound of water. The complete absence of any transition exhausts me on their behalf, for if there is anything I loathe *afterward*, or at least *immediately afterward*, it is having to move. Whatever the selfishness of preserving the warmth of a mouth that has nothing more to receive. [. . .]

Your devoted
Marcel Proust

LETTER 07
SEXATIONALLY YOURS
Mae West to Alfred Kinsey
March 1949

Born in New Jersey in 1894, sexologist Alfred Kinsey gained worldwide fame thanks to the publication of two revolutionary books, known collectively as the Kinsey Reports – the first, Sexual Behavior in the Human Male, published in 1948; the second, Sexual Behavior in the Human Female, in 1953 – in which, thanks to research gleaned from thousands of interviews, the sexual behaviours and predilections of the general public were laid bare. The books were highly controversial for their time and provoked endless debate and criticism. They also led to mountains of feedback in the form of letters, including this one, written by Hollywood actress and playwright Mae West.

THE LETTER

My dear Dr. Kinsey:—

I have never been frightened of sex. My saying that
might get a laugh because, as an actress, I'm so
thoroughly established as a sex personality that I
am often accused of being capable of injecting
double-entendre into a simple request for a cup of
coffee. So again, and meaning it—I have never been
frightened of sex. Instinctively, I suppose, I have
always felt sex to be what your report shows it to
be—a kind of standard equipment of the human
species, without which man might just as well be a
mollusk or an amoeba. (I checked those two, and
they're dull characters.)

The sexual behavior of human males does not
surprise me. Neither will sexual behavior in the
human female, as you report it.

Some years ago I tried to report a few truths
about that kind of behavior myself, in a play I wrote
and starred in, called, frankly enough, SEX . . .

I have been reporting on sex from time to time,
ever since. Our approaches to and handling of the
subject are different, but both of us are out in the
open about it. Your approach is scientific,
observing, investigating, classifying, statistical. Mine
involves at least the first two of those methods, but,

when it comes to statistics, I'm afraid the only figure I employ is my own. And that figure, which has become internationally familiar, stands for sex—just as your report of facts and figures does.

Sex is the basis of life and everybody is interested in it either consciously or unconsciously. It has been the basic theme of all my plays and pictures, and my characterizations symbolize the same. Because I portray sex with humor and good nature instead of something shameful, I think my portrayals are accepted in the spirit in which I play them. I have excited and stimulated, but I have never demoralized.

I feel as an actress and playwright I have been frank and honest in dealing with the subject—as I know you have been as a scientist. I cannot see sex as a tragedy in human life except, of course, in those cases where a psychiatrist—or actual restraining from sex violence of one sort or another—is needed. But I believe the more we are prepared to accept sex in our lives without a distorting sense of guilt and fear the less tragic will be any of its consequences.

A large portion of your book is devoted to presenting startling facts as to the amazing percentage of homosexuality in the total male population. In the same year I produced my play

SEX, I also wrote and produced a play I called THE DRAG. This dealt seriously with the problem of the homosexual in modern society, and it was well received by thinking and forward-looking people. However, it carried a message a little too premature for the general public.

Elsewhere in your book I find that you give a "third possible interpretation of sex as a normal biological function acceptable in whatever form it is manifested."

I am afraid that right here I'm going to have to object to any interpretation of sex that looks upon it as a mere "biological function." Any man (or woman) who has anything but ice water trickling through his arteries does not want to think of sex in any terms that do not include the psychology of romance, the mystery of allurement, the excitement and adventure of discovering the unknown in the personalities of those he chooses to love.

We should know everything about ourselves, but it is wiser (for sex's sake) not to know everything about each other. We should not be so exposed to each other, so common to each other, that sex becomes a mere commodity to be handed around like a pack of cigarettes.

How honest can we get about sex? I suppose it would be dangerous to admit that, at its best, sex is fun. But I would hasten to add that, at its worst, sex is self-destructive and criminal. There must be a happy medium—a common ground—where sex can meet with self-respect and unite to produce peace of mind for every individual.

Since one must be able to live in harmony with oneself before being able to live in harmony with others, the sooner one draws up an accounting of the sexual needs of one's character (privately, of course), the sooner will one be able to arrive at a sane and workable balance.

I would be the last to encourage uncontrolled sexual activity, licentiousness, in anyone. Obviously, early and thorough sex education and intelligent and sympathetic religious guidance are needed to enable men and women to accept and adjust the patterns of their sex lives so they may experience their basic human needs with dignity and self-respect.

Perhaps, Dr. Kinsey, you will say that all this doesn't sound much like Mae West talking—not the Mae West of the worldwide publicized sex personality. It happens to be Mae West thinking out loud. Your book about men, you know? I found it stimulatin'!

Sexationally yours,
Mae West

'I SUPPOSE IT WOULD
BE DANGEROUS TO
ADMIT THAT, AT ITS
BEST, SEX IS FUN.'
— Mae West

LETTER 08
THIS ASTONISHING PILGRIMAGE
John Cheever to his lover
1980

John Cheever was a celebrated novelist and master of the short story, a collection of which, The Stories of John Cheever (1978), won both the Pulitzer Prize for Fiction and the National Book Critics Circle Award. He was born in 1912 in Quincy, Massachusetts, and in 1941, aged twenty-eight, married Mary Winternitz, with whom he had three children. When Cheever died in 1982, his son Benjamin read through the letters his father had left behind, revealing a man he hadn't fully known; one who had embarked on numerous affairs with both women and men. In 1988, Benjamin Cheever edited and published a collection of his father's correspondence that hid very little and revealed a lot.

THE LETTER

Dear ____,
I woke this morning with a hard wet cock and it's
wet now after talking with you but this isn't all of
it; it's talking about the impossibility of teaching
and writing and happily eating a New York Steak at
a place called the firehouse where the lavish salad
bar consists of iceberg heels and pickled chickpeas
and laughing and throwing snowballs and you
complaining about my tobacco cough and the size
of my cock and you driving back to ____ with me
in the back seat disguised as laundry. I have
thought for a year that such love must be perverse,
cruel and inverted but I can find no trace of this
in my love for you. It seems as natural and easy as
passing a football on a fine October day and if the
game bores you you can toss me the ball and walk
off the grass and there will be no forlornness. Both
your short life and my long life have been, it
seems to me, singular adventures and to hold your
nice ass in my hands and feel your cock against
mine seems to be a part of this astonishing
pilgrimage.

I want your soft balls, I want to take off your glasses, I want your ass, your laughter and your loving mouth.

Love,
John

'I WANT YOUR ASS,
YOUR LAUGHTER AND
YOUR LOVING MOUTH.'

— John Cheever

DO NOT THINK I REJOICE IN BEING SEXLESS
Dora Carrington to Mark Gertler
16 April 1915

English painter Dora Carrington was born in 1893. Her artistic flair was evident from an early age, and in 1910 she attended art school in London, where she met Mark Gertler, a fellow artist who fell for her instantly and with great intensity. A romance blossomed, but the relationship was troubled and uneven, Gertler's passion unmatched by Carrington. In 1915, with Gertler increasingly frustrated by Carrington's refusal to sleep with him, she sent him this letter. At the top, capitalised here, Carrington had pasted a passage from a recent letter of Gertler's, to which she wished to respond.

THE LETTER

Hurstborne Tarrant

16 April 1915

NEXT LETTER, WHEN YOU WRITE, WHENEVER
YOU DO DON'T MENTION OUR SEX TROUBLE ETC
ETC ETC: *AT ALL* I AM HEARTILY SICK OF IT –
JUST WRITE AND TELL ME ABOUT YOURSELF THE
COUNTRY AS USUAL. AND IF EVER I WRITE
ABOUT IT TO YOU, *PLEASE* TAKE NO NOTICE.

OUR FRIENDSHIP IS NO WORSE OR BETTER
THAN ANY OTHER FRIENDSHIP. AT ANY RATE WE
ARE INTERESTED IN EACH OTHER – ENOUGH.
WHY SHOULD WE FUSS?

I WANT *SIMPLY* YOUR *FRIENDSHIP* AND *COMPANY*
MORE THAN ANYTHING IN THE WORLD.

You wrote these last lines only a week ago, and
now you tell me you were '*hysterical and insincere*'.
When you talked to me about it at Gilbert's and
said you loved my friendship were you hysterical
and insincere? Yes I know that your real love is
"beautiful and not low". Do not think I ever
doubted that.

Only I *cannot* love you as you want me to. You
must know one could not do, what you ask, sexual

49

intercourse, unless one does love a man's body. I have never felt any desire for that in my life: I wrote only four months ago and told you all this, you said you never wanted me to take any notice of you when you wrote again; if it was not that you just asked me to speak frankly and plainly I should not be writing. I do love you, but not in the way you want. Once, you made love to me in your studio, you remember, many years ago now. One thing I can never forget, it made me inside feel ashamed, unclean. Can I help it? I wish to God I could. Do not think I rejoice in being sexless, and am happy over this. It gives me pain also. Whenever you feel you want my friendship and company, it will always be here. You know that. This is all I can say.

REMEMBER THAT I WOULD SACRIFICE ALL FOR YOU, MY VERY LIFE IF YOU ASKED IT OF ME.

You write this — yet you cannot sacrifice something *less than your life* for me. I do not ask it of you. But it would make me happy if you could. Do not be angry with me for having written as I have. And please do not write back. There can be nothing more to say. Unless you can make this one sacrifice for me. I will do everything I can to be worthy of it.

'I DO LOVE YOU, BUT NOT IN THE WAY YOU WANT.'

— Dora Carrington

LETTER 10
SEX DOES NOT THRIVE ON MONOTONY
Anaïs Nin to the Collector
1940s

In the 1940s, Anaïs Nin and a collective of other writers earned $1 per page writing erotic fiction for the private consumption of an anonymous client known only as the Collector. Nin wrote a passionate letter to this mysterious figure and made known her frustrations – frustrations caused by his repeated insistence that they 'leave out the poetry' and instead 'concentrate on sex'.

THE LETTER

Dear Collector: We hate you. Sex loses all its power and magic when it becomes explicit, mechanical, overdone, when it becomes a mechanistic obsession. It becomes a bore. You have taught us more than anyone I know how wrong it is not to mix it with emotion, hunger, desire, lust, whims, caprices, personal ties, deeper relationships which change its color, flavor, rhythms, intensities.

You do not know what you are missing by your microscopic examination of sexual activity to the exclusion of others, which are the fuel that ignites it. Intellectual, imaginative, romantic, emotional. This is what gives sex its surprising textures, its subtle transformations, its aphrodisiac elements. You are shrinking your world of sensations. You are withering it, starving it, draining its blood.

If you nourished your sexual life with all the excitements and adventures which love injects into sensuality, you would be the most potent man in the world. The source of sexual power is curiosity, passion. You are watching its little flame die of asphyxiation. Sex does not thrive on monotony. Without feeling, inventions, moods, no surprises in bed. Sex must be mixed with tears, laughter, words, promises, scenes, jealousy, envy, all of the spices of fear, foreign travel, new faces, novels, stories, dreams, fantasies, music, dancing, opium, wine.

How much do you lose by this periscope at the tip of your sex, when you could enjoy a harem of discrete and never-repeated wonders? Not two hairs alike, but you will not let us waste words on a description of hair; not two odors, but if we expand on this, you cry "Cut the poetry." Not two skins with the same texture, and never the same light, temperature, shadows, never the same gesture; for a lover, when he is aroused by true love, can run the gamut of centuries of love lore, What a range, what changes of age, what variations of maturity and innocence, perversity and art, natural and graceful animals.

We have sat around for hours and wondered how you look. If you have closed your senses upon silk, light, color, odor, character, temperament, you must be by now completely shriveled up. There are so many minor senses, all running like tributaries into the mainstream of sex, nourishing it. Only the united beat of sex and heart together can create ecstasy.

Anaïs Nin

LETTER 11
THE LAST SEXUAL TABOO
J.M. Coetzee and Paul Auster
April 2009

Early in 2009 American author Paul Auster sent a copy of his thirteenth novel to J.M. Coetzee, the South African Nobel Prize-winning novelist, with whom he had been corresponding since 2008 on all manner of subjects. Their exchange of letters was compiled in Here and Now: Letters, 2008–2011 *and published in 2013. The novel Auster had sent to his new penpal was titled* Invisible: *a four-part story concerning a man named Adam Walker who, at one juncture, has an incestuous encounter with his sister, Gwen. Or so he believes. After reading the book, Coetzee wrote to Auster. Auster soon replied.*

THE LETTERS

Dear Paul,

Thank you for sending me *Invisible*, which I read in two long sessions—two gulps, as it were.

You told me last November that there would be incest in your next book, but I didn't appreciate—given the added complication you introduce, namely the question *Where does the act of incest take place, in the bed or in the mind or in the writing?*—how close to the heart of the book incest would be.

It's an interesting subject, incest, one to which I have not given much conscious thought until now (how would one dare to deny, post Freud, that one has not given it unconscious thought?). It strikes me as curious that, even in the popular tongue, we use the same denomination for sex between brother and sister as for sex between father and daughter or mother and son (let's put aside the various homosexual combinations for the moment). It's hard to experience the same frisson of repugnance about the first as about the latter two. I don't have a sister, but I find it all too easy to imagine how alluring sex games might be to a brother and a sister of more or less the same age—sex games proceeding to more than sex games, as in your book. Whereas sex with one's own offspring must seem quite a step to take. I would have thought we would have developed different terms for two very different moral acts.

There was a case last year in rural South Australia in which a father-daughter couple who had been living for decades as man and wife in fairly isolated circumstances were prosecuted. I don't remember all the details, but the court ordered that they be separated, the father/husband being enjoined not to come anywhere near his daughter/wife under threat of a jail term. It seemed to me a cruel punishment, given that the complaint had come not from either of the partners but from neighbors.

Having sex with one's parents or children must be just about the last sexual taboo that survives in our society. (I confidently predict that *Invisible* will not be greeted with howls of outrage, confirming my sense that brother-sister sex is OK, at least to talk about and write about.) We have come a long way from societies divided into castes within which sexual relations had to be confined. I suppose that the arrival of easy contraception marked the demise of sexual taboos: the bugaboo that the woman might give birth to a monster lost its force.

Not enough attention has been given, I think, to the role that the lore of animal husbandry played in the creation of sexual and racial taboos—lore dictating what species might be allowed to mate with what other species, or within a bloodline how many degrees of separation there had to be, evolved in the course of hundreds of generations of stock raising.

Anyway, today pretty much everything seems to go. The righteous fury that used to be able to play over a whole range of tabooed sex acts (including adultery!) has been focused on a single act, namely grown men having sex with children, which is, I suppose, our way of extending the coverage of the father-child taboo.

Interesting that when in benighted corners of the world (most notably benighted corners of the Muslim world) adulterous couples are punished, we criticize the law that punishes them for ignoring their human rights. What kind of world are we living in in which it is our *right* to break a taboo? What is the point of having a taboo (your Byronic Adam Walker might ask) if it is OK to violate it?

All the best,

John

Dear John,

So happy that Invisible reached you and that you
have consumed it so quickly.

No, I haven't given much conscious thought to
the subject of incest either—at least not until I
wrote the novel. Unlike you, I do have a sister, but
she is nearly four years younger than I am, and the
thought of going down that road with her never
once crossed my mind. On the other hand, when I
was eighteen or nineteen, I dreamed one night that
I was making love to my mother. The dream baffled
me then and continues to baffle me today, since it
seems to demolish the classic Freudian equation:
sublimation of desires through cryptic symbols and
often oblique imagery, each thing standing in for
something else. His theory has no place for what I
experienced. As I recall, I was not disturbed by
what was happening inside the dream, but after I
woke up I was shocked and revolted.

Shocked because at bottom I suppose I accept
the taboo as inviolate. Not just incest between
parents and children but between brother and sister
as well. Whether what happens in my book with
Walker and Gwyn really happens is open to question, but I had to write those passages from a

position of absolute belief, and I confess that it was difficult for me—as if I had cut through the barbed-wire fence that stands between sanity and the darkness of transgression. And yet I fully agree with you that the book will not be met with howls of outrage (at least not on that count!). In fact, I think I already have proof of that. Earlier this week, Siri and I did a joint reading at Brown University in Providence at the invitation of Robert Coover (an old friend whom we hadn't seen in a while). I read some pages from the second part (which included the "grand experiment" but not the full-bore incest of 1967), and although Siri reported that some students tittered nervously behind her, after the reading was over not a single person mentioned those paragraphs. "Nice reading," they said, or "Very interesting, can't wait to read the book," but nothing about the content of what they had heard.

Bouncing off your remarks about animal husbandry, I was reminded of a book I translated many years ago by the French anthropologist Pierre Clastres—*Chronicle of the Guayaki Indians*—an excellent, beautifully written study of a small, primitive tribe living in the jungles of South America. There is one homosexual in the group, Krembegi, and this is the astonishing account of what person(s) he can sleep with—and why:

The ultimate bases of Atchei (Guayaki) social life are the alliances between family groups, relations that take form and are fulfilled in marriage exchanges, in the continual exchange of women. A woman exists in order to circulate, to become the wife of a man who is not her father, her brother, or her son. It is in this manner that one makes Picha, allies. But can a man, even one who exists as a woman, "circulate?" How could the gift of Krembegi, for example, be paid back? This was not even imaginable, since he was not a woman, but a homosexual. The chief law of all societies is the prohibition against incest. Because he was kyrypy-meno—(literally, an anus-lovemaker)—Krembegi was outside this social order. In his case, the logic of the social system—or, what amounts to the same thing, the logic of its reversal—was worked out to its very end: Krembegi's partners were his own brothers. 'Picha kybai (meaning kyrypy-meno) menoia.' "A kyrypy-meno man does not make love with his allies." This injunction is the exact opposite of the rules governing the relations between men and women. Homosexuality can only be "incestuous"; the brother sodomizes his brother, and in this metaphor of incest the certainty that there can never be any real incest (between a man and a woman) without destroying the social body is confirmed and reinforced.

Extraordinary, no? Encouraging incest in order to discourage it. The head spins . . .

On another note, I want to congratulate you on your piece for the *New York Review* on Beckett's letters. Thorough, compassionate, and just. Siri was especially pleased by the space you devoted to Bion. In the wake of your article and in anticipation of the talk I have agreed to deliver in Ireland this coming September, I dutifully plowed through the book, and now that I have come to the end, I want to revise my earlier comments to you. It is not boring. Far from it, and what moved me most was to watch his slow and painful evolution from an arrogant, know-it-all prick into a grounded human being. A note to one of the last letters (the book is not in front of me, so my wording might be off) quotes a letter from Maria Jolas to her husband in which she says something like: Beckett is better now—implying, I think, that they never cared for him personally and were now beginning to change their opinion.

And yes, the notes represent an extraordinary

undertaking. But do we really have to be told that Harpo Marx's real name was Arthur?

Best thoughts,
Paul

LETTER 12
OBLIVION OF WORDS
Frida Kahlo to Diego Rivera
Undated

Born in 1907, Mexican painter Frida Kahlo was twenty years old when she first met fellow artist Diego Rivera. He was twenty-one years older than Kahlo and already married for a second time by that point. However, that didn't stop them embarking on a wildly passionate, turbulent and often troubled affair that would last until Kahlo's death in 1954 and see them marry each other on two occasions. When she wasn't making art, Kahlo loved to write to Rivera. Many of those letters have survived. In her posthumously published diaries, this particularly fervent example can be found, undated, addressed to her lover, sprawled across eight pages in her handwriting.

THE LETTER

My Diego:

Mirror of the night.

Your eyes green swords inside
my flesh. waves between
our hands.
All of you in a space full of
sounds – in the shade and in the
light. You were called AUXO-
CHROME the one who captures color. I
CHROMOPHORE – the one who gives color.
You are all the combinations
of numbers. life.
My wish is to understand lines
form shades move-
ment You fulfill and I receive.
Your word travels the entirety of
space and reaches my cells
which are my stars then goes to
yours which are my light.

Ghosts.

Auxochrome – Chromophore

It was the thirst of many years re-
strained in our body. Chained
words which we could not
say except on the lips of dreams.
Everything was surrounded by the green miracle of the landscape of your body.
Upon your form, the lashes of the
flowers responded to my touch, the murmur
of streams. There was all manner of fruits
in the juice of your lips, the blood
of the pomegranate, the horizon
of the mammee and the purified pineapple.
I pressed you against my breast
and the prodigy of your form penetrated all my blood through
the tips of my fingers. Smell
of oak essence, memo-
ries of walnut, green breath
of ash tree. Horizon and land-
scapes = I traced them with a kiss.
Oblivion of words will form
the exact language for
understanding the glances of
our closed eyes.
= You are here, intangible
and you are all the universe which
I shape into the space of my

room. Your absence springs
trembling in the ticking of the
clock, in the pulse of light;
you breathe through the mirror. From
you to my hands, I caress
your entire body, and I am with
you for a minute and I am with
myself for a moment. And my
blood is the miracle which
runs in the vessels of the air
from my heart to yours.
WOMAN. xxxxxxxxxxxxx
xxxxxxxxxxxxxxxxx
MAN. xxxxxxxxxxxx
The green miracle of the landscape
of my body becomes in you the
whole of nature. I fly
through it to caress the rounded
hills with my fingertips,
my hands sink into the
shadowy valleys in an urge to
possess and I'm enveloped in the embrace
of gentle branches, green
and cool. I penetrate the sex of
the whole earth, her heat
chars me and my entire body
is rubbed by the freshness of the tender

leaves. Their dew is the sweat
of an ever-new lover.
It's not love, or tenderness, or
affection, it's life itself, my
life, that I found what I saw it
in your hands, in your month and
in your breasts. I have the taste of
almonds from your lips in my
mouth. Our worlds have
never gone outside. Only one
mountain can know the core of
another mountain.
Your presence floats for a moment or two
as if wrapping my whole
being in an anxious wait
for the morning. I notice that I'm
with you. At that instant
still full of sensations,
my hands are sunk
in oranges, and my body
feels surrounded by your
arms.

For my Diego,
the silent life giver
of worlds, what is
most important is the nonillusion.

morning breaks, the
friendly reds, the big
blues, hands full of leaves,
noisy birds, fingers
in the hair, pigeons' nests
a rare understanding of
human struggle simplicity
of the senseless song
the folly of the wind in my
heart = don't let them rhyme girl
= sweet *xocolatl* [chocolate] of ancient
Mexico, storm in the
blood that comes in through the
mouth − convulsion, omen,
laughter and sheer teeth needles
of pearl, for some gift on a seventh of July, I
ask for it, I get it, I sing,
sang, I'll sing from
now on our magic − love.

LETTER 13
YOU'RE FOOD AND DRINK TO ME
Henry Miller to Anaïs Nin
30 July 1932

In 1932, months after first meeting in Paris and despite both being married, celebrated Cuban diarist Anaïs Nin and Henry Miller – the hugely influential novelist responsible for writing the sexually explicit (for the times) novel Tropic of Cancer *(1934), which Nin helped to finance – began a fiery love affair. The liaison would last for many years, a situation further intensified by the fact that Nin also had an openly discussed affair, albeit brief, with Miller's then-wife, June, as their own romance grew. Such explosive conditions resulted in countless passionate love letters from both parties. This particular missive was written prior to a heated few days at Nin's home in France.*

THE LETTER

Anaïs:

[. . .] I think I have discovered a title for the book.
How do you like either of these—"Tropic of
Cancer" or "I Sing the Equator." (2nd volume
would be "Tropic of Capricorn." The last book
ought to be just "God.")

This evening at sunset I lay on my couch and
watched the clouds sailing by my window. You can
see nothing but the clouds when you lie there and
clouds are wonderful when they are punctured by
cerulean blue. (Time and Space—what these things
are beginning to mean to me. I'm just waking up!)
There was one blue hole about eight lightyears
away into which a sparrow dove. I was intoxicated
by it. Why is it that distance in itself is so
enchanting?

Sunday morning and no letter from Anaïs.
Desperate. Is it possible you didn't receive the big
letters I mailed? One of them was sealed, the other
was about of equal size—I think I have sent you
about three thick ones, this will make the fourth.

[. . .]

When you return I am going to give you one

literary fuck fest—that means fucking and talking and talking and fucking—and a bottle of Anjou in between—or a Vermouth Cassis. Anaïs, I am going to open your very groins. God forgive me if this letter is ever opened by mistake. I can't help it. I want you. I love you. You're food and drink to me—the whole bloody machinery, as it were. Lying on top of you is one thing, but getting close to you is another. I feel close to you, one with you, you're mine whether it is acknowledged or not. Every day I wait now is torture. I am counting them slowly, painfully. I don't know when you return—the 7th or the 15th? But make it as soon as you can. Be unselfish—yes, I am asking you to. Make a sacrifice. I need you. This long Sunday—*how will I ever get through it?* It is just killing time. Tomorrow there may be a letter. Everything hangs on tomorrow. God, I want to see you in Louveciennes, see you in that golden light of the window, in your Nile-green dress and your face pale, as frozen pallor as of the night of the concert. Let the hair wave—expose it to the sun—let the color return. I love you as you are. I love your loins, the golden pallor, the slope of your buttocks, the warmth inside you, the juices of you. Anaïs, I love you so much, so much! I am getting tongue-tied. I am even crazy enough to believe that you

might walk in on me unexpectedly. I am sitting
here writing you with a tremendous erection. I feel
your soft mouth closing over me, your leg
clutching me tight, see you again in the kitchen
here lifting your dress and sitting on top of me
and the chair riding around over the kitchen floor,
going thump, thump.

Henry

LETTER 14
YOUR LOVELY HAMPTON WICK
Cynthia Albritton to Keith Richards
2 August 1965

Since 1968, when she and her best friend famously
sought out and made a plaster cast of Jimi Hendrix's
penis, legendary groupie Cynthia Albritton (a.k.a.
Cynthia Plaster Caster) has been immortalising rock
stars' members – and, since 2000, breasts – in plaster
for the world to see. Quite successfully, too, as
evidenced by the exhibitions, documentary film, tribute
songs and autobiography that have followed. In 1965,
three years before getting the first yes from Hendrix,
Cynthia wrote an admiring letter to Keith Richards in
an ultimately unsuccessful attempt to introduce herself.
It was reprinted in Stanley Booth's book The True
Adventures of The Rolling Stones.

THE LETTER

Dear Keith,
We watched you on the TV the other night and the
first thing that grabbed our eyes was your lovely
Hampton Wick. After that we did little besides
studying it. We're not kidding; you've got a very
fine tool, as a friend of ours puts it. From the way
your pants project themselves at the zipper, we
figure you've got a beauty of a rig. Sometimes
we hoped you'd whip it out or something, but they
don't have TV cameras that could focus on anything
that large, do they? Hey, tell Mick he doesn't have
to worry about the size of his either; we noticed
that already (well, who could help but?). Our
favorite names for you are Keith the Giant Meat
and Hampton Mick.

Keith, we're serious; we judge boys primarily by
their Hamptons because they're so exciting to look
at and contribute so much to a healthy relationship.
We can hardly wait till you come into town in
November, maybe then we can find out more about
what's inside your pants.

We hope you don't think we ought to receive
head treatment or be put away before we attack

men or something. We hope you sympathize with us and agree that sex should be openly appreciated just like all other works of beauty and ingenuity. We like to say that we really think while other people just sit there all cringed and inhibited inside, afraid they'd offended someone if they told them something complimentary about their Hamptons or, as in your case, their shoulder boulders.

Would you like to write us back and confirm our beliefs about your Hampton Wick? Would you say, aside all the humility, that it is as spectacular as your pants have lead [led] us to believe? Do you always wear your rig on the right side because you're right handed or doesn't it make any difference? What is the first thing YOU look for in GIRLS?

If you're interested, drop by awhile, why don't you, when you're in Chicago or give us a ring. We're both 18 and like to wear tight-fitting sweaters. We think a girl should wear things tight on top to please a boy, and that a boy should do the same at the bottom to please us.

So please don't forget to answer us. And keep pleasing us by wearing those pants good and tight.

Reach us at:

Cynthia Plastercaster

Chicago, Ill.

LETTER 15
THERE ARE NO NICE CUSTOMERS
Tanja Rahm to her former customers
January 2014

Tanja Rahm was twenty years old when she entered the world of prostitution and began life as a sex worker in Denmark. For three long years, Rahm worked in various Danish brothels, eventually escaping what had become a miserable existence with invaluable help from her family. Rahm went on to train as a therapist and sexologist in Køge, south of Copenhagen. In 2014, she wrote this letter to her former customers.

THE LETTER

Dear sex customer,
If you think that I ever felt attracted to you, you are terribly mistaken. I have never had any desire to go to work, not once. The only thing on my mind was to make money, and fast. Do not confuse that with easy money, it was never easy. Fast, yes. Because I quickly learned the many tricks to get you to come as quickly as possible, so I could get you off of me, or from under me, or from behind me.

And no, you never turned me on during the act. I was a great actress. For years I have had the opportunity to practice for free. Actually, it falls under the concept of multi-tasking. Because while you lay there, my thoughts were always elsewhere. Somewhere where I was not confronted with you sucking out my self respect, without spending as much as ten seconds on the reality of the situation, or to look me in the eye.

If you thought you were doing me a favour by paying me for 30 minutes or an hour, you were wrong. I would rather have had you in and out as fast as possible. When you thought yourself to [be] my holy saviour, asking what a pretty girl like me was doing in a place like that, you lost your halo when you proceeded to ask me to lie down on my back, and then put all your efforts into feeling my body as much as possible with your hands. Actually, I would have preferred if you had just laid on your back and had let me do my job.

When you thought you could boost your masculinity by getting me to climax, you need to know that I faked it. I could have won a gold medal in faking it. I faked it so much the receptionists would nearly fall off of their chairs laughing. What did you expect? You were perhaps number three, or number five, or eight that day. Did you really think I was able to get turned on mentally or physically by having sex with men I did not choose myself? Not ever. My genitals were burning. From lubricant and condoms. And I was tired. So tired, that often I had to be careful not to close my eyes for fear of falling asleep while my moaning continued on autopilot.

If you thought you paid for loyalty or small talk, you need to think again. I had zero interest in your excuses. I did not care that your wife had pelvic pain, and that you just could not go without sex. Or when you offered any other pathetic excuse for coming to buy sex with me. When you thought I understood you and had sympathy for you, it was all a lie. I had nothing but contempt for you, and at the same time you destroyed something inside of me. You sowed the seeds of doubt in me. Doubt as to whether all men were just as cynical and unfaithful as you were.

When you praised my appearance, my body, or my sexual abilities, you could just as well have vomited on me. You did not see the person behind the mask. You only saw that which confirmed your illusion of a raunchy woman with an unstoppable sex drive. In fact, you never said what you thought I wanted to hear. Instead, you said what you yourself wanted to hear. You said that which was needed to preserve your illusion, and which prevented you thinking about how I had ended up where I was at twenty years of age. Basically you did not care at all. Because you had one goal only, and that was to show off your power by paying me to use my body as it pleased you.

When a drop of blood appeared on the condom, it was not because my period had just come. It was because my body was a machine, one that could not be interrupted by a monthly cycle, so I inserted a sponge into my vagina when I menstruated. To be able to continue on the sheets. And no, I did not go home after you had finished. I continued working, telling the next customer exactly the same story that you had heard. You were all so consumed with your own lust that a little menstrual blood did not stop you.

When you came with objects, lingerie, costumes or toys, and wanted erotic role-play, my inner machine took over. I was disgusted with you and your sometimes quite sick fantasies. The same goes for the times when you smiled and said that I looked like a seventeen-year-old girl. It did not help that you yourself were fifty, sixty, seventy, or older.

When you regularly violated my boundaries by either kissing me, or inserting your fingers into me, or taking off your condom, you did it knowing perfectly well that it was against the rules. You were testing my ability to say no. And you enjoyed it when I did not object clearly enough, or when I too often would simply ignore it. And then you used it in a perverted way to show how much power you had and that you could cross my boundaries. When I finally told you off, and made it clear that I would not have you as a customer again if you could not respect the rules, you insulted me. You were condescending, threatening and rude.

When you buy sex, it says a lot about you, your humanity, and your sexuality. To me, it is a sign of your weakness, even though you confuse it with a sick sort of power and status. You think you have a right. I mean, the prostitutes are out there anyway, right? But they are only prostitutes because men like you stand in the way of healthy and respectful relationships between men and women. Prostitutes exist only because men like you feel you have the right to satisfy your sexual urges using the orifices of other people's bodies. Prostitutes exist because you and your peers feel that your sexuality requires access to sex whenever it suits you. Prostitutes exist because you are a misogynist, and because you are more concerned with your own sexual needs than relationships in which your sexuality could actually flourish.

When you buy sex, it reveals that you have not found the core within your own sexuality. I feel sorry for you, I really do. That you are so mediocre that you think that sex is all about ejaculating into a stranger's vagina. And if one is not handy, it is never further away than down the street, where you can pay an unknown woman to be able to empty yourself into a rubber while inside of her. What a petty and frustrated man you must be. A man unable to create profound and intimate relationships where the connection runs deeper than just your ejaculation. A man, who expresses his feelings through his climaxes, who does not have the ability to verbalise them, but prefers to channel them through his genitals to get rid himself of them. What a weak masculinity. A truly masculine man would never degrade himself by paying for sex.

As far as your humanity goes, I believe in the good in people, also in you. I know that deep down you have a conscience. That you have quietly wondered whether what you did was ethically and morally justifiable. I also know that you defend your actions and likely think that you treated me well, were kind, never mean or did not violate my boundaries. But you know what? That is called evading your responsibility. You are not confronting reality. You delude yourself in thinking that the people you buy are not bought. Not forced into prostitution. Maybe you even think that you did me a favour and gave me a break by talking about the weather, or giving me a little massage before you penetrated me. It did me no favours. All it did was confirm to me that I was not worth more. That I was a machine, whose primary function was to let others exploit my sexuality.

I have many experiences from prostitution. They enable me to write this letter to you. But it is a letter which I would much rather not have written. These are experiences I wish I could have avoided.

You of course you thought of yourself as one of the nice customers. But there are no nice customers. Just those who confirm the women's negative view of themselves.

Take my hand and see me for the person I am on the inside. Let us go together to make a difference in the future. Let us raise our voices to our friends, our girlfriends, our business associates, our bosses, our politicians, and last but not least, to the prostituted. Let us raise our voices together and say that sex is private. Let us shout that sex is not a product on a shelf, but that it can cost dearly if it is treated as one. Let us scream to the world that money and sex do not belong together, and that sex belongs to all together different and mutually reciprocal relationships. Because in this case, you will re-concur my respect and I will see you as the person you are, and not just as a buyer of sex, seduced by an illusion.

Yours truly,
Tanja Rahm

'LET US RAISE OUR
VOICES TOGETHER AND
SAY THAT SEX IS
PRIVATE.'
— Tanja Rahm

LETTER 16
MY BODY SHALL BE ALL, ALL YOURS
Radclyffe Hall to Evguenia Souline
24 October 1934

*Poet and author Radclyffe Hall (often 'John' to her
loved ones) was born in Bournemouth, England, in
1880, and is best known for her lesbian novel* The Well
of Loneliness. *When published in 1928, the book broke
new ground and led to a British court judging it as
'obscene' due its supposedly 'unnatural practices
between women'. All copies of the book were to be
destroyed, and in fact it remained out of print in the
UK until 1949, six years after Hall's death. It has since
sold millions of copies worldwide. In 1934, despite
living with long-term partner Una Troubridge, Hall met
and fell in love with a Russian nurse named Evguenia
Souline and, to Troubrudge's dismay, embarked on an
intensely passionate affair. This letter was sent late
that year. The three women eventually lived together in
Italy.*

THE LETTER

My beloved and moja radost[1]. By now you will
know that I have written again and why I did not
write for three days—I simply dared not write,
heart of my being. This letter will not be a very
long one, but I wrote yesterday before leaving Rye,
though the post will not reach you so soon from
the country.

[. . .]

Darling—I wonder if you realize how much I
am counting on your coming to England, how
much it means to me—it means all the world, and
indeed my body shall be all, all yours, as yours will
be all, all mine, beloved. And we two will lie close
in each others arms, close, close, always trying to
lie even closer, and I will kiss your mouth and your
eyes and your breasts—I will kiss your body all
over—And you shall kiss me back again many
times as you kissed me when we were in Paris. And
nothing will matter but just we two, we two
longing loves at last come together. I wake up in

---

1 A Russian term of endearment suggesting 'greatly
   cherished'.

the night & think of these things & then I can't
sleep for my longing, Soulina. This is love—make
no mistake about it—love has come to you—you
are loved and loved. No one whom you meet is
more loved than you are—no one in the whole
world can be more loved. When you look at people
you can say to yourself in your heart—"I also has
[sic] got a lover—I am loved until the love is as
pain, as a scourge of whips on my lover's back, as
a fire that torments and consumes my lover."
Blessed is this lover that torments day and night,
night & day, for it also illumines and sustains when
the loved one is kind—be kind, then, my Soulina.

Your John

LETTER 17

MAN'S BEST FRIEND? A SHEEP? A HORSE?

Jessica Mitford to the *New York Times* Book Review

8 April 1992

In March 1992, in response to a bill under considera-
tion by the Senate Judiciary Committee which would, if
passed, 'encourage victims of sexual crimes to bring
civil suits against publishers and distributors of material
that is "obscene or constitutes child pornography"',
novelist and screenwriter John Irving wrote a piece for
the New York Times. *In it, he criticised any such action*
which could shift the responsibility for a sexual crime
away from its perpetrator. He also, more generally,
complained of increasing levels of censorship. A week
later, a letter was sent to, and printed in, the same
paper, written by English author Jessica Mitford.

THE LETTER

Oakland
April 8, 1992

To the Editor:

John Irving's article (March 29, 1992) on pornography was a brilliant effort. I especially enjoyed his comments about cause and effect—whether there are fewer incidents of women being force-fed eels in Canada as a consequence of "The Tin Drum" being banned in that country?

Consider Amsterdam, acknowledged porn capital of the Western World, where you can't walk downtown without being assaulted on every side by filthy, absolutely revolting, movie marquees offering everything the most rotten heart could desire in the way of dirty films; sex shops, with God knows what for sale; porn bookshops and so on.

Yet Amsterdam claims to be freer of crimes of assault against women than any Western city. Why? One theory is that would-be rapists act out their fantasies by watching the dirty movies, reading the dirty books. (I don't pretend to know if this is true—it has a sort of spurious sounding logic, possibly dreamed up by the Amsterdam Chamber of Commerce. But let that pass.)

Further on cause and effect, I do remember being fascinated by the Kinsey Report on the sexual habits of the American male, in which we learned that one out of every eight American men has had intercourse with animals. At any large party, I couldn't help glancing around to try and guess which of the men had done it—and with whom? Man's best friend? A sheep? A horse? The report was disappointingly reticent on this score. Have the Animal Rights advocates been heard from on this subject? For is it not possible that a reader of the Kinsey Report might become so titillated as to have a go with a pig, just to see what it's like?

Yours truly,

Jessica Mitford

LETTER 18
MAX STANDBY
Dian Fossey to Robinson McIlvaine
22 January 1979

In 1963, having learnt Swahili and studied primatology,
thirty-one-year-old Dian Fossey left her home in
Kentucky and travelled to Nairobi, Kenya, to begin
studying endangered mountain gorillas in their natural
habitat. In 1967 she founded the Karisoke Research
Center in Rwanda to further her studies. Fossey's
invaluable work continued until her death in 1985,
and in 1988 her story became a Hollywood movie,
based on her 1983 memoir, Gorillas in the Mist. *Living*
in a mountain forest for months on end presented
problems for Fossey, as evidenced by this amusing
letter from Rwanda, in which she announced the death
of a battery-powered 'close friend' she named Max
Standby. The letter's recipient, Robinson McIlvaine, was
the President of the African Wildlife Foundation.

THE LETTER

January 22nd, 1979

Dear Rob,

I really received some bad news today. A close
friend of mine, actually I only really got to know
him well on three occasions, died after a lingering
illness, as yet not properly diagnosed.

Perhaps you know him, as he was fairly well-
known in conservation circuits; his name was Max
Standby. Apparently he had some kind of electrical
pacemaker, and when that started to fail, there was
no place in Rwanda to get it fixed, so he just
sweated it out until the end.

I do admire the pluck he showed, but I can't tell
you how much I miss him. He was one of those
you thought you could always rely on in time of
need. I can't understand why all the good guys
have to go first.

As ever,
Dian

LETTER 19
A POTENTIALLY LIMITLESS SHARED ECSTASY

Frederick B. Exner, M.D., to the *Journal of the
American Medical Association*
June 1950

*In June 1950, an article on the subject of frigidity
appeared in the peer-reviewed* Journal of the American
Medical Association *which stated, amongst other things,
that 'normal' women should be passive during sexual
intercourse. It provoked this letter, written by noted
radiologist and lecturer Frederick B. Exner.*

THE LETTER

To the Editor:– The article by Kroger and Freed on "Psychosomatic Aspects of Frigidity" in THE JOURNAL, June 10, page 526, is deserving of high praise. Nevertheless, it contains statements I must challenge.

In the first paragraph on page 529, under "Diagnosis of Frigidity," the statement "The woman has absolutely no control over the muscles involved in these involuntary contractions" is contrary to the facts. Some women do and some do not have such control, just as some can and some cannot wiggle their ears. In each case there is some reason to believe that most could learn such control if they set out to do so.

I also criticize the last full sentence in the first column on page 528: "The 'normal' woman, during the sex act, should be passive and receptive of the penis." Here is the enthronement of personal prejudice as "normality" and "morality" that is the banc of most writing on sex and that the balance of the article has largely avoided. Moreover, it seems completely out of keeping with the implied premise of the entire article, namely, that it is "good" that the woman derive as complete gratification as possible from the sex act.

The quoted statement is even less acceptable if the golden rule is taken as the basic ethic of the sexual relationship. The act then becomes a truly cooperative enterprise wherein neither wishes to derive pleasure at the expense of the other. Creating a mutually enjoyable experience becomes the objective of each, and no rules apply except that whatever is done be safe for both and enjoyed by both. It is a mistake to identify either activity or aggressiveness with pleasure.

The act, so performed, consists of appeal and response, offer and acceptance, enticement, surprise, suspense, all achieved by constantly shifting aggressiveness and passivity, activity and relaxation on the part of each partner. When successful, the pleasure to each from pleasing the other becomes so intermingled with the pleasures of being pleased and of knowing that the partner wants to please, that they become indistinguishable. Each type of pleasure reacts with and reinforces the others to build up a potentially limitless shared ecstasy.

In like manner, and in these circumstances, the physical and the spiritual components of pleasure react on and reinforce each other, building to intensities of both that are beyond the comprehension of those who think in terms of how the "normal" person "should" perform the act.

I am convinced that, within the limitations imposed by the rights of potential offspring, the sole basis of sexual ethics is that same golden rule that is the only sound basis for any social relationship.

F. B. EXNER, M.D., Seattle.

EVEN MY BONES SEEM TO CRY FOR YOU
Georgia O'Keeffe to Alfred Stieglitz
16 May 1922

Distinguished American painter Georgia O'Keeffe and photographer Alfred Stieglitz wrote more than 5,000 letters to each other during their thirty-year relationship. The love affair began in 1917, shortly after they met: Stieglitz, despite already being married, was smitten. By the 1920s they were both at the top of their professions – she as an innovative artist, he as a photographer and promoter of art, O'Keeffe's included – and as their bond deepened, their letters intensified. This one was penned in 1922, two years before they married following Stieglitz's divorce.

THE LETTER

Dearest I love you—
I am on my back—wanting to be spread wide
apart—waiting for you—to die with the sense of
you—the pleasure of you—the sensuousness of you
touching the sensuousness of me—All my body—
all of me is waiting for you to touch the center of
me with the center of you—

I got up—a moment after writing the last
page—walked round the room—found the other
pages of my letter to you—looked out the
window—

Dearest—my body is simply crazy with wanting
you—If you don't come tomorrow—I don't see
how I can wait for you—I wonder if your body
wants mine the way mine wants yours—the
kisses—the hotness—the wetness—all melting
together—the being held so tight that it hurts—the
strangle and struggle—the release that moans and
groans and the quickly drawn breath—the reaching
of something in the whole body for the center of
heaven—the relaxing to prolong the pleasure that
goes through every inch of one's body—one's

center touched—repeatedly with that center that goes into one's center with such madness pushing and pounding and beating at the middle of one's soul till it is satisfied—the ring about the opening to one's center begins to contract and one becomes gradually a limp thing—hot—wet—relieved—satisfied—and your smooth wet little pinkness lies beside me—all in a limp dampness—both unconscious in his release—for a moment—then pale little smiles at one another—

When I feel how your touching my body—getting into my body—has given all of me to you—all of you to me as much as one human being can get into and feel another of another—I wonder if there is any difference in body—and spirit—soul and mind— aren't they all one and the same thing—

I seem to feel my body very intensely this morning—so much so that I wonder if there is anything else to me—It's my body that wants you and it seems to be the only thought or desire that I have—It even seems to be my only memory of you—two bodies that have fused—have touched with completeness at both ends making a complete circuit—making them one—a circle that nothing can break—You have given me—the circle of the most painfully intense pleasure—most pleasurably intense pain—The circle with two centers—each touching the other—The mathematical impossibility of the situation is probably nature's reason for the particularly keen pleasure she affords when the mathematically impossible happens—

I must work—I'm in such a state that I could write about this all day—

Does it tell you how wildly hungry every inch of me is for you—even my toes. It's no use to say it's my soul crying for you—I know good and well that it is my body—my blood—my flesh—even my bones seem to cry for you—hunger for you—

Love—

G—

LETTER 21
YOUR NAME IS UPON EVERY TONGUE
Pope Pius II to Rodrigo de Borja
11 June 1460

*In June of 1460, news reached Pope Pius II of an orgy
which had recently taken place in the gardens of
Giovanni di Bichis's palace in Tuscany. To his dismay, it
had been attended, and to some extent organised, by
the vice-chancellor of the Roman Church, Cardinal
Rodrigo de Borja – a notoriously sinful member of the
disgraced Borgia family – whose uncle, Pope Callixtus
III, had died two years earlier. This calm but furious
letter was the Pope's response. Thirty-two years later,
Rodrigo de Borja was elected Pope Alexander VI.*

THE LETTER

Dear Son,

Four days ago several ladies of Siena who are
entirely given up to worldly frivolities were
assembled in the gardens of Giovanni di Bichis.
We have heard that you, unmindful of the high
office with which you are invested, were with
them from the seventeenth to the twenty-second
hour. In company with you was one of your
colleagues, whose years, if not the respect due
to the Holy See, ought to have recalled to him
his duty. From what we have heard, the most
licentious dances were indulged in; no amorous
seductions were lacking, and you conducted
yourself in a manner wholly worldly. Modesty
forbids the mention of all that took place, for not
only the acts themselves, but their very names,
are unworthy of your position. In order that your
lusts might have freer course, the husbands,
fathers, brothers, and kinsmen of the young
women were not admitted. You and a few servants
were the organisers of this orgy. To-day every one
in Siena is talking about your frivolity, which is
the subject of common derision. Certain it is that
here at the Baths, where there is a large number
of ecclesiastics and laymen, your name is upon

every tongue. Our displeasure is beyond words, for your conduct has brought discredit upon your holy office and state; people will say that they invest us with riches and greatness, not that we may live a blameless life, but that we may have means to gratify our passions. This is why the princes and the Powers despise us and the laity mock us daily; this is why our own conduct is thrown in our face when we reprove others. The Vicar of Christ is exposed to contempt because he appears to tolerate these proceedings. You, dear son, have charge of the bishopric of Valencia, the most important in Spain; moreover, you are Chancellor of the Church, and, what makes your conduct all the more reprehensible, is your having a seat among the Cardinals, with the Pope, as adviser of the Holy See. We submit the case to your own judgment: is it becoming for a man of your position to pay court to young women, to send fruit and wines to those whom you love, and to have no thought during the whole day save for all kinds of voluptuous pleasures? We are blamed on your account, and the memory of your blessed uncle, Calixtus, likewise suffers, and he is condemned by many for having heaped honour upon your head. It is useless to seek to excuse yourself on account of your age; you are no longer so young as not to be able to understand what duties your dignities impose upon you. A cardinal ought to be above reproach and an example of good living to all. Have we the right to be vexed when temporal princes bestow disrespectful titles upon us, when they dispute the possession of our property and force us to submit to their injunctions? It must be confessed that we inflict these wounds upon ourselves, and that with our own hands we prepare these troubles, by every day diminishing the authority of the Church through our conduct. Our punishment for it in this world is dishonour, and in the world to come well-merited torment. May, therefore, your good sense put restraint upon irregularities, and may you never lose sight of the dignity with which you are clothed, that you may never again be called a gallant among women and young men. If this occurs again we shall be obliged to point out that it is in spite of our admonitions, and that it causes us great pain. In such a case our censure would cover you with confusion. We have always loved you and thought you worthy of our protection as a man of modest and serious character. Therefore, conduct yourself in such a way that we may retain this opinion of you; nothing could contribute further to this than the adoption of a regular mode of life. Your age, which is not such as to preclude amendment, authorises us to admonish you thus paternally.

Petriolo,

June 11, 1460

'FROM WHAT WE HAVE HEARD, THE MOST LICENTIOUS DANCES WERE INDULGED IN, NO AMOROUS SEDUCTIONS WERE LACKING . . .'

– Pope Pius III

LETTER 22
AT LENGTH THE WAVES GREW MORE TERRIFIC
Rupert Brooke to James Strachey
10 July 1912

In January 1912, following years of anxiety caused by homosexual impulses and the recent rejection from Katherine 'Ka' Cox, the woman with whom he wished to spend his life, English war poet Rupert Brooke suffered a severe nervous breakdown. Months later, as he recovered, Brooke learnt of the death of Denham Russell-Smith, the man he had lost his virginity to in 1909. He wrote this letter to friend James Strachey the next day and described the experience. Brooke died at sea three years after this letter was sent, having been poisoned by an insect bite as he headed for the Battle of Gallipoli.

THE LETTER

Wednesday night
July 10, 1912

[. . .] How things shelve back! History takes you
to January 1912 — Archaeology to the end of
1910 — Anthropology to, perhaps, the autumn of
1909. —

The autumn of 1909! We had hugged & kissed
& strained, Denham & I, on & off for years — ever
since that quiet evening I rubbed him, in the dark,
speechlessly, in the smaller of the two Small Dorms.
An abortive affair, as I told you. But in the summer
holidays of 1906 & 1907 he had often taken me
out to the hammock, after dinner, to lie entwined
there. — He had vaguely hoped, I fancy . . . But I
lay always thinking [of] Charlie [Lascelles].

Denham was though, to my taste, attractive. So
honestly and friendlily lascivious. Charm, not
beauty, was his *fate*. He was not unlike Ka, in the
allurement of vitality & of physical magic. — oh,
but Ka has beauty too. — He was lustful, immoral,
affectionate, & delightful. As romance faded in me,
I began, all unacknowledgedly, to cherish a hope
. . . But I was never in the slightest degree in love
with him.

In the early autumn of 1909, then, I was glad to get him to come & stay with me, at the Orchard. I came back late that Saturday night. Nothing was formulated in my mind. I found him asleep in front of the fire, at 1.45. I took him up to his bed – he was very like a child when he was sleepy – and lay down on it. We hugged, & my fingers wandered a little. His skin was always very smooth. I had, I remember, a vast erection. He dropped off to sleep in my arms. I stole away to my room: & lay in bed thinking – my head full of tiredness & my mouth of the taste of tea & whales, as usual. I decided, almost quite consciously, I *would* put the thing through the next night. You see, I didn't at all know how he would take it. But I wanted to have some fun, &, still more, to see what it was *like*, and to do away with the shame (as I thought it was) of being a virgin. At length, I thought, I shall know something of all that James & Norton & Maynard & Lytton know & hold over me.

of course, I *said* nothing.

Next evening, we talked long in front of the sitting room fire. My head was on his knees, after a bit. We discussed Sodomy. He said he, finally, thought it *was* wrong . . . We got undressed there, as it was warm. Flesh is exciting, in firelight. You must remember that *openly* we were nothing to each other – less even than in 1906. About what one is with Bunny (who so resembles Denham). Oh, quite distant!

Again we went up to his room. He got into bed. I sat on it & talked. Then I lay on it. Then we put the light out & talked in the dark. I complained of the cold: & so got under the eiderdown. My brain was, I remember, almost all through, absolutely calm & indifferent, observing progress, & mapping out the next step. Of course, I planned the general scheme beforehand.

I was still cold. He wasn't. "Of course not, you're in bed!" "Well then, you get right in, too." I made him ask me – oh! without difficulty! I got right in. Our arms were round each other. "An adventure!" I kept thinking: And was horribly detached.

We stirred and pressed. The tides seemed to wax . . . At the right moment I, as planned, said "Come into my room, it's better there . . ." I suppose he knew what I meant. Anyhow he followed me. In that large bed it was cold; we clung together. Intentions became plain; but still nothing was said. I broke away a second, as the dance began, to slip my pyjamas. His was the woman's part throughout. I had to make him take his off – do it for him. Then it was purely body to body – my first, you know!

I was still a little frightened of his, at any too sudden step, bolting; and he, I suppose, was shy. We kissed very little, as far as I can remember, face to face. And I only rarely handled his penis. Mine he touched once with his fingers; and that made me shiver so much that I think he was frightened. But, with alternate stirrings, and still pressures, we mounted. My right hand got hold of the left half of his bottom, clutched it, and pressed his body into me. The smell of the sweat began to be noticeable. At length we took to rolling to & fro over each other, in the excitement. Quite calm things, I remember, were passing through my brain. "The Elizabethan joke 'The Dance of the Sheets' has, then, something in it." "I hope his erection is all right" . . . and so on. I thought of him entirely in the third person. At length the waves grew more terrific; my control of the situation was over; I treated him with the utmost violence, to which he more quietly, but incessantly, responded. Half under him & half over, I came off. I think he came off at the same time, but of that I have never been sure. A silent moment: & then he slipped away to his room, carrying his pyjamas. We wished each other "Good-night." It was between 4 & 5 in the morning. I lit a candle after he had gone. There was a dreadful mess on the bed. I wiped it clear as I could, & left the place exposed in the air, to dry. I sat on the lower part of the bed, a blanket round me, & stared at the wall, & thought. I thought of innumerable things, that this was all; that the boasted jump from virginity to Knowledge seemed a very tiny affair, after all; that I hoped Denham, for whom I felt great tenderness, was sleeping. My thoughts went backward & forward. I unexcitedly reviewed my whole life, & indeed the whole universe. I was tired, and rather pleased with myself, and a little bleak. About six it was grayly daylight; I blew the candle out & slept till 8. At 8 Denham had to bicycle in to breakfast with Mr Benians, before catching his train. I bicycled with him, and turned off at the corner of –, is it Grange Road? –. We said scarcely anything to each other. I felt sad at the thought he was perhaps hurt & angry, & wouldn't ever want to see me again. – He did, of course, & was exactly as ever. Only we never referred to it. But that night I looked with some awe at the room – fifty yards away to the West from the bed I'm writing in – in which I Began; in which I "copulated with" Denham; and I felt a curious private tie with Denham himself.

So you'll understand it was – not with a *shock*,

for I am far too dead for that, but with a sort of
dreary wonder and dizzy discomfort – that I heard
Mr Benians inform me, after we'd greeted, that
Denham died at one o'clock on Wednesday
morning, – just twenty four hours ago now.

Rupert

'FLESH IS EXCITING IN
FIRELIGHT.'

— Rupert Brooke

LETTER 23
THE POOR-WHORES PETITION

Madam Cresswell and Damaris Page to Lady
Castlemaine

25 March 1668

*For several days over the Easter period in 1668, thou-
sands of London's apprentices took part in the Bawdy
House Riots. This annual event saw young men, armed
with weapons, damage and loot the city's brothels and
assault its prostitutes. In response, a group of sex
workers, led by noted brothel-keeper Elizabeth
Cresswell, drafted this satirical letter and sent it to the
lover of King Charles II, Lady Castlemaine. No response
was forthcoming.*

THE LETTER

The Poor-Whores Petition.
To the most Splendid, Illustrious, Serene and
Eminent Lady of Pleasure, the
Countess of CASTLEMAINE, &c.
The Humble Petition of the Undone Company
of poore distressed Whores,
Bawds, Pimps, and Panders, &c.

Humbly showeth,
That Your Petitioners having been for a long time
connived at, and countenanced in the practice of
our Venerial pleasures (a Trade wherein your
Ladyship hath great Experience, and for your
diligence therein, have arrived to high and Eminent
Advancement for these last years), But now, We,
through the Rage and Malice of a Company of
London-Apprentices, and other malicious and very bad
persons, being mechanick, rude and ill-bred Boys,
have sustained the loss of our Habitations, Trades
and Employments; And many of us, that have had
foul play in the Court and Sports of *Venus*, being
full of Ulcers, but were in a hopeful way of
Recovery, have our Cures retarded through this
Barbarous and Un-*Venus*-like Usage, and all of us
exposed to very hard shifts, being made uncapable

of giving that Entertainment, as the Honour and Dignity of such persons as frequented our Houses doth call for, as your Ladyship by your own practice hath experimented the knowledge of.

We therefore being moved by the imminent danger now impending, and the great sense of our present suffering, do implore your Honour to improve your Interest, which (all know) is great, That some speedy Relief may be afforded us, to prevent Our Utter Ruine and Undoing. And that such a sure Course may be taken with the Ringleaders and Abetters of these evil disposed persons, that a stop may be put unto them before they come to your Honours Pallace, and bring contempt upon your worshipping of *Venus*, the great Goddess whom we all adore.

Wherefore in our Devotion (your Honour being eminently concerned with us) We humbly judge it meet, that you procure the *French*, *Irish*, and *English Hectors*, being our approved Friends, to be our Guard, Aid, and Protectors, and to free us from these ill *home bread* slaves, that threaten your destruction as well as ours, that so your Ladyship may escape our present Calamity, Else we know not how soon it may be your Honours Own Case: for should your Eminency but once fall into these Rough hands, you may expect no more Favour then they have shewn unto us poor Inferior Whores.

Will your Eminency therefore be pleased to consider how highly it concerns You to restore us to our former practice with Honour, Freedom, and Safety; For which we shall oblige ourselves by as many Oaths as you please, To Contribute to *Your Ladyship*, (as our Sisters do at *Rome & Venice* to his *Holiness the Pope*) that we may have your Protection in the Exercise of all our Venerial pleasures. And we shall endeavor, as our bounden duty, the promoting of your Great Name, and the preservation of your Honour, Safety and Interest, with the hazzard of our Lives, Fortunes, and HONESTY.

And your Petitioners shall
(as by custom bound)
evermore Pray, etc.

Signed by Us, Madam Cresswell and Damaris Page, in the behalf of our Sisters and Fellow-Sufferers (in this day of our Calamity) in Dog and Bitch Yard, Lukeners Lane, Saffron-Hill, Moor-fields, Chiswell-Street, Rosemary-Lane, Nightingale-Lane, Ratcliffe-High-way, Well-Close, East-Smithfield etc., this present 25th day of March 1668.

LETTER 24
I WAS A MASTURBATOR'S MASTURBATOR
Dalton Trumbo to Christopher Trumbo
8 November 1958

*Oscar-winning screenwriter Dalton Trumbo began
working for the Hollywood studios in the 1930s, then
in his twenties. His rise was swift, and by the 1940s,
with a number of hits behind him, he was one of the
industry's highest-paid writers. Fast-forward to 1950
and Trumbo was serving eleven months in prison and
blacklisted, having refused to testify before the US
House Committee on Un-American Activities. When
released, he wrote dozens more screenplays using a
pseudonym, including* Spartacus *in 1960. Two of those
movies won Academy Awards for their scripts. But
most importantly, above all else, in 1958 he wrote this:
an epic, amusing, seemingly endless letter to his son in
which he expounded on the benefits of masturbation.*

THE LETTER

Los Angeles, California
November 8, 1958

My dear son:

I have at hand your most recent letter addressed, I
believe, both to your mother and to me. That
portion which I assume was designed to capture
my attention has. I refer to your addled account
of an exchange between you and Mike [Butler]
relative to mensal checks from home. You may be
sure I shall give it much thought.

You also inform us you haven't made holiday
travel reservations because you haven't the money
to pay for them. Artful fellow! Do you truly think
me so stupid as to send the fare directly to
you, who'd only squander it in high living and
end up stranded on Christmas Eve begging poor-
man's pudding in some snow-swept Bowery
breadline?

The procedure is this: go at once to an airline
office and make round-trip reservations (not
deluxe, not a milk-run either). Do it immediately,
for the seasonal rush is already at hand. Notify me
of the airline, flight number, date and hour of
arrival and within twenty-four hours a check made

over to the airline will be delivered into your greedy fist. Take it to the seller and the deal is consummated without laying you open to temptation.

I am sending you two books I think appropriate for a young man spending five-sevenths of his time in the monkish precincts of John Jay Hall. The first is *Education of a Poker Player*, by Henry O. Yardley. Read it in secret, hide it whenever you leave quarters, and you'll be rewarded with many unfair but legal advantages over friend and enemy alike, not to mention that occasional acquaintance who has everything including money.

The second book I think you should share with your young companions. It is *Sex Without Guilt*, by a man who will take his place in history as the greatest humanitarian since Mahatma Gandhi, Albert Ellis, Ph.D. This good man has written what might be called a manual for masturbators. That is to say, in one slim volume he has clarified the basic theory of the thing, and then, in simple layman's language, got right down to rules and techniques. This in itself is a grand accomplishment; but what most compels my admiration is the zest, the sheer enthusiasm which Dr. Ellis has brought to his subject. The result (mailed in plain wrapper under separate cover) is one of those fortuitous events in which the right man collides with the right idea at precisely the right time. It makes a very big bang indeed.

It is Dr. Ellis' idea to spring masturbation from the bedroom's crepusculine gloom, where for endless generations it has lain a saprogenic curse on millions of little lechers, and turn it loose in the parlor where it rightfully belongs. This chap doesn't find anything wrong with it at all: indoors or out, he ranks it right up there with ping-pong, gin rummy and "Maverick" as a time-honored, health-giving, red-blooded patriotic pastime.

What Ellis wants to do − and by gad he does it, too! − is remove that gnawing sense of guilt so characteristic of the act, the awful tension of it, the leering, searing, sneering fear of it. (Oh Phalloform, dread Phallio / Let never me deride / My onanistic, irresistic, post-pubescent bride!) Once all that unhealthy brooding is dissolved, nothing remains of a former vice but unadulterated fun. And that's what Ellis is after. He doesn't want American youth to go about guilt-twitching like a pack of inbred Chihuahuas for nothing more serious than a raging appetite for fescenninity. He doesn't want those golden hours of childhood festered over with concern about the imminent putrefaction of genitalia. He wants young people not to give a damn! He wants them to relax. He wants, in short, a world of happy masturbators.

This whole new approach – this fresh wind blowing under the sheets, so to speak – this large-hearted appeal for cheerful self-pollution, invokes perhaps a deeper response in my heart than in most. For I (sneaky, timorous, incontinent little beast with my Paphian obsessions) was never wholesomely at home with my penile problem, nor ever found real happiness in working it out – all because of that maggoty, mountainous pustule of needless guilt that throbbed like an abscess in my young boy's heart.

On warm summer nights while exuberant girl-hunting contemporaries scampered in and out of the brush beneath high western stars, I, dedicated fool, lay swooning in my bed with no companion save the lewd and smirking demons of my bottomless guilt. Cowering there in seminal darkness, liquescent with self-loathing, attentive only to the stealthy rise and Krafft-Ebbing of my dark scrotumnal blood, fearful as a lechwe yet firmer of purpose than any rutting buffalo, I celebrated the rites of Shuah's son with sullen resignation. Poor little chap on a summer's night, morosely masturbating . . . !

There were lads in Grand Junction, Colorado

(most of whom became civil servants or evangelistic clergymen) who strode the sunlit streets of that never-to-be-forgotten town like fierce young gods, lean and supple, tall and strong, pace brisk, shoulders well thrust back, frank of face, forthright of smile, clear of eye, innocent of heart, clean of mind. But I was not one of them.

Oh no, not I. Not your poor father.

When I appeared in public, toad-blinking against the unwonted and revelatory blaze of day, I conveyed the immediate impression of ambulant filth – of obscenity, so to speak, in transit. I lurched through those years like some demented crab, shoulders at a goatish hunch, eyes a-scum with fantasies of defloration, my acneous skin (hot with crimson shames) exuding from every greasy pore that sour effluvia which marks imagined love. My sweaty nippers – ah, cursed, cursed paws! – I carried thrust to the very bottom of my trouser pockets, in which humid and forbidden depths they secretly envaginated that marvelous little pendant I knew must drop from its frazzled moorings the instant I withdrew my helping hands.

I turned thin and pale; my odor changed from sour to stercoraceous; reflexes vanished altogether; palpitations of the heart set in, accompanied by giddy spells and sudden faints. My left eye developed so fearsome a tic that its aftermath may be seen to this day in the crapulous squint with which you are perhaps far too familiar. My blood ceased to coagulate: for eleven months I went about completely swathed in bandages. Satyriasis, ever latent in my yielding genes, turned chronic and then acute: treatment consisted in the rapid alteration of ice packs with cauldrons of scalding water. I was placed on a diet of loblolly laced with seaweed extract.

It was this revolting dish even more than my rampageous libido that brought my nervous system to a state of utter dissolution. I would start up briskly at the slightest sound and begin to canter counterclockwise, and in ever widening circles, crepitating all the while like a Percheron at close trot (you know that horrid sound thup-thup-thup-thurp-thup), and nickering suspiciously. I became unhinged that the mere sight of a girl reduced me to mucilaginous pulp identifiable as human only by a pair of inflamed eyes and a faint squinking sound that seemed to proceed from the hepatized heart of the mess. Ah, sweet suppurating soul of Satan, I thought I never would get adjusted!

Even now, more than three decades later (and I, as you know, a power of moral strength, a civic leader, a respected – nay, beloved – unity figure), even now when I forget a friend's name, or lay my spectacles, or pause in mid-sentence idiocy (my thought having died twixt concept and delivery) – even now such lapses set a clammy chill upon my heart, while purulent memories of my secret shame incarnadine the sallow of these aging cheeks.

It's then, while panic tightens my sagging throat, that I whisper to myself: "It's true after all. It does make you crazy. It does cause the brain to soften. Why, oh why did I like it so much? Why didn't I stop while I was still ahead of the game? Was it only one time too many that caused this rush of premature senility? Or a dozen times? Or a thousand? Ah well – little good to know it now: the harm's done, the jig's up, you're thoroughly raddled, better you'd been born with handless stumps."

An instant later I blessedly recall the name, I find the spectacles, complete the sentence – and the salacious ghoul of my sickened fantasies retreats once more into the shadows, not banished to be sure but held off at least for a few more days or hours. I ask you, boy – if the mere memory of past guilt has such power to swoon my adult mind, can you imagine the effect upon a naturally depraved constitution of what then was present guilt?

I recall a certain chill winter night on which my father took me to one of those Calvinist fertility rites disguised as a father-and-son banquet. I was in no real shape to mingle with respectable society, being then at the dismal nadir of my lechery and much given to involuntary belching, squirching, belly-rumbling, wind-breaking, nasal pearl-diving and the like. The banquet consisted of dead fish, stale bread, soft-boiled potatoes and leather-bottomed pie.

Master of the revels was an acrid old goat named Horace T. McGuiness who kept a doxy, engaged in brutish orgies, and reserved his public hours for denunciation of everything dear to a little boy's heart. This excrementitious old fornicator was greatly venerated in our town, and much in demand for such festivities as that which I describe.

He buttoned his protruberant vest on discs of decayed egg yolk and brayed like Balaam's ass voiding hot barbed-wire. His nostrils extruded threads of ductile mucus which streamed down-ward in gay opalescent loops to a scraggle of brush which concealed practically all of that moist, pink, vulviform cave of the winds that served him as a mouth. When speaking – and he always spoke – he displayed the carious ruin of what in his youth had been a gaggle of strong yellow teeth. With every phrase he emitted dense clouds of sewer gas, while his harsher consonants shot forth such poisonous showers of spittle that full-grown bull blowflies fell stunned to the tablecloth the instant they flew in range.

The old debauchee opened his discourse with a series of blasphemous demands that the Almighty agree with his ghastly notions and make our young minds (his whole talk was addressed to us youthlets, never to pa) receptive to the bilge he proposed to pump into them. Then he got down to the meat of the program which, to no one's surprise, was girls. When you go out with a young lady, he slavered, you go out with your own sister. As you treat her, so will your sister be treated. It followed that you must not think of it in relation to her, you must not suggest it to her, and certainly you must not do it to her. If you did, you were a blackguard, a degenerate, a runnion, a cullion, and a diddle-cove.

To this day I don't know why that crazed old rake's clapper-claw affected me as it did. I was a menace only to myself. For all the harm I was able to do girls, or they me, their whole concupiscible tribe had just as well been my sisters. On the other hand, it seemed plain to me that if one day I did burst upon the world as the hymeneal Genghis

Khan of my dreams, I'd be in for an extremely incestuous time of it.

Several winters later, when my headmaster at McTeague's Chicago Academy for Distraught Boys, enraged by the nocturnal racket of my solitary revels, clapped hands on me and dragged my quaking hulk to a lupanar much favored by the faculty, I stood spellbound and terrified as the grisettes paraded for my selection. The vile, incestuous objurgations of old Reek-mouth still fevered my brain. These girls were my sisters – the tall one over there, and the tiny one with the dazzling blue curls, and that charming creature with the wise clitorial wink (the first I'd seen to that time) – all of them sisters! How could I even think of them that way?

Piteously I tried to explain the taboo that held me apart from this naked herd of mooing female relatives. Headmaster (he was a goodhearted man but quick with his right) cuffed me about for something under an hour. Toward the end of the beating I was enabled to see the thing from headmaster's point of view rather than that of old Stench-tooth. I began to regard the lovely denizens of that establishment with rising interest. My heart grew light. My temples ceased to throb. My eyes began to glitter brilliantly. I found myself laughing, as Columbus must have laughed when first he spied the shimmered green of Hispaniola.

Ah-ha, my darlings – no sisters ye nor brother I, blessed be the sapient gods! (Descend, Murgatoyd!) Flee for your lives, thou still unravished brides of quietness – thou foster children of slow time! (Down, slavering monster!) Weep, ye Sabine maidens – cringe, ye moaning seraphim! (*Abajo*, little Sir M!) That which ye greatly feared has come upon you! The stuprator is at hand! *Estoy aqui! Me voici! Adsum!*

I learned, so to speak, the hard way. (Ah, Chicago, Chicago – stud-barn of the western world!) Not once in those three wild aphrodisiacal weeks did headmaster or I set foot outside that house of ecstasy. We ordered the telephone disconnected, and had our meals sent in piping hot from the Pump Room. I, who had barely matriculated, qualified for graduate work in three fiery days. When finally we returned to the vertical world (headmaster, being without tenure, lost his appointment at the Academy, while I, poor lad, was sent down for simple venery) I was a new boy: snake-lean, rock-hard and fero-ciously determined that earth herself should reel beneath the measured thunder of my copulations. That, however, is a different story to be reserved for later times and nicer problems. Returning now to that atrocious hugger-mugger which set me thus to dreaming: -

Having deranged our building psyches with this sister business, old Pus-head passed on to the subject of procreation – or, more precisely, non-procreation. In unbelievable detail he shambled through the story of Judah, son of Jacob, son of Abraham (nee Abram), son of Terah, son of Nahor, son of Serug, son of Reu, son of Peleg, son of Eber, son of Salah, son of Axpharaxed, son of Enoch, son of Jared, son of Mahalalcel, son of Cainan, son of Enos, son of Seth, who was born to Adam and Eve in their autumnal years.

Now to the story. Judah had three sons improbably named Er, Onan and Chezib. Er caroused so heroically that "the Lord slew him," making of his wife Tamar a widow. Judah there-upon commanded his second son, this Onan chap, to marry his brother's relict and have children by her. Onan yielded to the first command and moved in with the girl (note how that sister theme creeps in again?), but he flatly refused stud service, devising instead an escape route that ensured his memory and made his name practically a household word to this day. He spilled his seed out onto the ground. (Hence onanism, onanistic, and the like, for you know what.)

By closing my mind and abandoning all sanity I can still hear that demented old reprobate howling his bill of particulars against poor Onan, shaking his fist at us all the while and sweating like a diseased stoat. "He wasted his seed! Oh monstrous, shameful, nameless act he spilled it right out into the ground! All of it! Yes sir, every last drabble of it! And this displeased the Lord. And the Lord slew him!" This ringing period he concluded with a gust of spittle so noxious that a waitress, caught in its mere fallout, sank fainting to the floor beneath a tray of priceless cut-glass fingerbowls.

Without even a sideglance at his gasping victim, old Sprue-tongue rushed on to a warning against the most dangerous period of a boy's day, which he leeringly defined as those last ten minutes before the coming of blessed sleep. This period, he rasped, was Onan's hour, that dread time of temptation which separated the men from boys. He commanded us, on pain of Onan's fate, as we loved God, loathed sin, and cherished our immortal souls, thenceforth to sleep with our hands outside the covers "until, in the unpolluted glory of young manhood, that chaste girl of your dreams appears on the transept of God's heaven to give you, through holy matrimony, that love which no man deserves and all desire." Whereupon we were ordered to rise en masse, lift high our swearing arms ("All the perfumes of Arabia will not sweeten this little hand!") and take the pledge.

Well. You can imagine how I felt, poor shuddering pertinacious masturbating little dolt! My young companions, their faces shining with devotion, rose like eager chipmunks to recite that preposterous oath as solemnly as if it were a Te Deum. I felt compelled to join them, my skin flushing beet-red beneath a field of yellow pimples then riotously in bloom from the base of my throat to the farthest border of my scaly scalp. Seated once more, I vomited softly into a cannister of caramels my father took with him wherever he went. As for father – from that time forward a murk, a dark estrangement rose between us. How could I, degraded sperm-wasting voluptuary that I was, ever again look squarely into the calm serenity of his grave sperm-thrifty eyes? I couldn't and never did. For us, that moment was the end.

When I went to bed that night the thermometer shivered at twenty-three degrees below zero. I slept alone in public, so to speak, an open porch with only a dismal flap of canvas to separate my quarters from those glacial winter winds that howled for three straight months each year on the other side of it. Shuddering like a greyhound bitch in heat, I burrowed beneath mounded covers. My congealing breath formed a beard of frost on the quilt beneath my chin. My pale hands, like twin sacrificial lambs, lay freezing outside the covers. It made no sense at all to me, yet I'd been gulled into taking their peccant oath, and now in my own dim-witted fashion I proposed to keep it. It was the witching hour.

While I lay there pondering Onan's fate, nerves twitching, gonaducts aflame, ten chilly digits convulsively plucking at my counterpane, I tried to divert my tumescent thoughts from their obsession. I thought on heroes and their heroism: on Perseus, Jason, Odysseus, Achilles – and it was on Achilles that I paused, evaluating again that dip in the Styx with only his left heel exposed. It occurred to me that the tragedy of his death stemmed directly from the triviality of the wound that brought him low.

At this point my incomparable flair for nastiness took charge. What would have happened, I asked myself, if Thetis had held the little tyke by his tippet instead of his heel? Since everyone understands there's utterly no point in living once your tassel's been shot off, all tears and sympathy would have been focused on that gory dopple, reducing his subsequent death to mere blessed anti-climax. The whole point of the yarn, it seemed to me, would have been changed, and for the better. Thus musing, I fell asleep. The next morning I was rushed off whooping to the hospital, brought low with quick pneumonia and seven frostbit claws. So much then, for keeping pledges.

There are still other stories I could tell you — tales of those corybantic pears that would inflame your bowels and thin your heart's young blood. They would, however, be merely cumulative: if my point isn't made by now it never will be. Yet the more I think on it the more positive I become that you will never truly be able to comprehend in all its horror that interminably sustained convulsion which was your father's youth. It's only reasonable that this should be so, since you've had so many advantages that were denied to me. To name but three of them — a private room, a masturbating father, and Albert Ellis, Ph.D.

Neither, I think, will you ever be able to understand that flood of savage joy which filled my heart on first reading *Sex Without Guilt*. I felt, with Keats, like "some watcher of the night skies. When a new planet swims into his ken." Having passed through such flaming pubic hells as would altogether carbonize a weaker lad, can anyone hope to imagine the wild surmise that stunned my soul on discovering that I'd been right all along? That all my Brobdingnagian juvenile debaucheries had been as innocent as so many taffy-pulls? That I was, in truth, an example and a martyr for all who'd gone before me and for endless millions still to come?

For that's what it amounts to, son. I carried the ball for all of us, and carried it farther than anyone had a right to expect. I was the Prometheus of my secret tribe – a penile virtuoso, a gonadic prodigy, a spermatiferous thunderbolt; in fine, a masturbator's masturbator. In that sad hour when you lay me away, remember with awe what I did, and carve those words in ageless granite above my resting place, that your sons and your sons' sons may not forget the blood of champions coursing through their veins.

I am still, as you may suspect, somewhat distraught from reliving for your instruction the calamitous tale of my youth. That it's been painful I can't deny, but what is pain compared to the immeasurable satisfaction of being a proper dad to you? I am also, perhaps, still too deeply under the literary and erotic spell of *Lolita*, which I've read four straight times in four straight days. If you don't know the book, you must get it at once. This chap Nabokov, like Dr. Ellis, is a way-shower, one of those spirits who understands that everything under the sun has its time and place and joy in an ordered world.

His description of a two-year Saturnalia between an aging pervert and a twelve-year-old female (a "nymphet," as Nabokov so charmingly describes young girls in the immediate stages of pre- and postpubescence) is something to make your mouth water. Now that *Lolita* has brought nymphetophilia into the world of fashion and made it, thank God, as respectable as ornithology, I'm willing to place it on record that my own sexual taste in young girls runs strongly to larvines, beside whom your average nymphet seems gross and dissolute. A larvine begins to glow at five-and-a-half and generally is quite hagged out before her eighth birthday. Perhaps it's the very brevity of her flower that so attracts me. The man fortunate enough to catch one of these delightful creatures at the very peak of larvineal bloom – provided, of course, no one catches him – will be rewarded indescribably.

A pair of them approach even as I pen these words. They live two houses down. I spy on them night and day with a 40-power Stankmeyer-Zeitz. They're on the point of passing my study door en route to Sunday school. One of them's already in the third grade. Soon she'll be too old. Closer and closer they come. My excitement mounted like the fires of Krakatoa.

Now (squish-squish-squish) they draw even with

the door. Glowing grandeur of tiny milk-fleshed thigh. Liquescent breath of gay vulvaginous pearl. (Psst! Speak to the nice old man. Come into my parlor. Ice cream? Candy? Morphine? Exciting photographs?) They continue down the drive. Patter of footsteps fainting with my heart. Nubescent rumplets winkling wild their nappled wonder. Scent of loinwine sighing, crying, dying on soft amber-tawny singing little legs. Oh my God —

Goodbye, boy!

DAD

I WAS THE WORST BED PARTNER IN FIVE CONTINENTS

Martha Gellhorn to Betsy Drake

3 September 1972

Martha Gellhorn was one of the greatest war correspondents in modern history. In December of 1936, in a bar named Sloppy Joe's in Key West, Florida, she met and fell for fellow writer Ernest Hemingway, and four years later they were married. Their union lasted five years. She later said of their sex life: 'My whole memory of sex with Ernest is the invention of excuses, and failing that, the hope that it would soon be over.' She married again in 1954, only for that partnership to dissolve seven years later. In 1972, with two divorces and numerous lovers behind her, Gellhorn wrote to good friend Betsy Drake and described her indifference to sex.

THE LETTER

September 3 1972
72 Cadogan Square
London SW1

Betsy dear,

. . . Four days after the N. Viets sadly and politely
refused me, they got in touch with MY paper (the
St. Louis Post-Dispatch) out of the blue, and gave a
visa to a man reporter. This is how Women's Lib
was born. I'd rightly touted the paper and made an
impassioned speech about their being idiots to take
applications in order; they needed every US
reporter they could get now, before the elections.
Well, anyhow, I educated them. It is a blow because
the man they've chosen, Dudman, is a good man,
but writes only with his feet; an opportunity lost.
However. I do not take my personal blows as hard
as I might since I am aware every minute of the
really horrendous blows falling on the innocent and
helpless everywhere, the Uganda Asians, the Jews in
Russia and all poor Vietnamese.

Now, back to love and sex; what a fascinating
topic. I don't know whether I'm prim; I sure
haven't lived it. I started living outside the sexual
conventions long before anyone did such dangerous

stuff and I may say hell broke loose and everyone thought unbridled sexual passion was the excuse. Whereas I didn't like the sex at all; I only believed in honesty and besides the man wanted it and what I wanted was to live at top speed, deep into French politics, picketing with strikers, racing before the Garde Mobile and bringing out a little French newspaper – maybe the first underground paper. I never ever thought you got something for nothing in this life, and fair's fair, and besides, all my life idiotically, I thought sex seemed to matter so desperately to the man who wanted it that to with-hold was like withholding bread, an act of selfishness. But myself, I was not 'awakened', if that's the word; often attracted, often horribly in love, but the bed part didn't come off – I think partly due to the clumsiness of the men and partly (largely?) due to a Victorian upbringing: sex and love were different. If I practised sex, out of moral conviction, that was one thing, but to enjoy it probably (in my subconscious) seemed a defeat. Anyway, I didn't; and envied those who did, realising it made life so much easier.

Besides that, I believe, but never know, that what has always really absorbed me in life is what is happening outside. I accompanied men and was accompanied in action, in the extrovert part of life;

I plunged into that; that was something altogether to be shared. But not sex; that seemed to be their delight and all I got was a pleasure of being wanted, I suppose, and the sort of tenderness (not nearly enough) that a man gives when he is satisfied. I daresay I was the worst bed partner in five continents. And the agile and experienced men were always shits, which didn't endear sex to me as you can imagine. So I just went on having abortions, because shits got me into them, and being wanted; but I never in my life looked at a man and said, that one is for me. So no, Betsy, there we are different; I cannot get myself into any state about a man who is ugly or badly made, which is a pity and a stupidity, but really, I am not even apt to think about sex until the actual event is transpiring, we have different imaginations. And so, obviously, I do not use men because there's nothing for me to use, I guess . . .

Also, if sex isn't the number one excitement, one gets bored or intellectually outraged much quicker. I fear I start with my head and go to my heart and finally end up in the genital region. But my lover, my last and only, was a great change; the first man who didn't make any effort to own me because, morally, he couldn't, he had no right even to try. And somehow, to my intense amazement, sex is fine with him, perhaps because I feel absolutely safe. But of course, it is hardly existent; it's not sex, it's like a Xmas present or an Easter present, a delight which rarely happens. He is different because of his name and life and position in the world; he has less freedom than Prince Philip. He has no time, no leisure, a shocking amount of money; all kinds of handicaps. No, I would never have married him; no, I would never have lived with him – nor, ever again, with anyone. Freedom is the most expensive possession there is; it has to be paid for with loneliness, of course, and self reliance; but I value it most. I would love to have a few weeks holiday with him, but never will. He is there; I know he feels something special for me as I do for him; and in those hours (it is often only hours) we can get, we are merry together. I forgive him all his ignorance of how real life is down here on the ground, because he is honest and kind, and he can't help not having enough imagination not to understand what he has never come anywhere near experiencing.

But I don't know what you are afraid of. A man cannot do anything more than disappoint you; he can't destroy you. Not like prison, which can destroy anyone. I've been driven nearly round the bend by both my husbands, but both were odd creatures (and of course, so am I) but never really round the bend and all I had to do was escape. No one can prevent a woman from running for her life. I don't understand fear; I understand lack of opportunity. The men don't grow on trees; any man won't do.

[. . .]

And now back to the mines and the extra hours worth of business and duty letters and then happily to bed. I am dieting and working at Kew; I am disgusted by nine extra pounds like a large sausage around my middle, sign of failed discipline, failed hope, I get fat from despair which is really the limit. Despair would be much pleasanter if it made one thin and interesting like *La Dame aux Camélias*.

See you in the US somehow. And do have a lovely autumn in Cambridge. Shall I bring you woollen underwear from London?

Always,

Martha

LETTER 26
I NEED TO RELIEVE MY SEXUALITY
PHYSICALLY SOMEHOW

Amrita Sher-Gil to Marie Antoinette Gottesmann
February 1934

*By the time of her death aged just twenty-eight,
pioneering Indian artist Amrita Sher-Gil had already
made her mark in the art world due to paintings such
as her piece* Young Girls *(1932), which saw her become
the youngest-ever painter to be awarded the Gold
Medal at Paris's Grand Salon. Born in 1913 to an
Indian father and Hungarian mother, she had been
living and studying in France since the age of sixteen.
She stayed until her return to India at the end of 1934.
This letter was written that year to her mother, who
had heard rumours that her daughter had embarked
upon a sexual relationship with a female friend and
fellow painter, Marie-Louise Chassany.*

THE LETTER

My dear Mummy,

Do you know that I am of age? So, please do respect me, my dear clever and understanding mother. Yesterday I received your letter that affected me like lightning from the clear sky . . . I never had any relationship with Marie Louise, and will not have one either. And you can believe me. Knowing how unprejudiced, objective and intelligent you are, I am going to be very frank with you. I confess that I also think as you do about the disadvantages of relationships with men. But since I need to relieve my sexuality *physically* somehow (because I think it is impossible to spiritualize, idealize sexuality *completely* in art, and channelizing it through art for a lifetime is impossible, only a stupid superstition invented for the brainless), so I thought I would start a relationship with a woman when the opportunity arises, and to be quite frank I myself thought that Marie Louise was of abnormal inclinations. Marie Louise is in fact not quite normal (it is enough to look at her art which is wonderful and interesting but sickly) but she is not a lesbian. She is a curious woman. I still do not know about her sexual life for she keeps on avoiding the subject or simply does not answer my questions. To sum up, we never had anything to do with each other in sexual terms, and I think that she does not have a sexual life (at least in the usual meaning of the word)! I think that she is the slave of some sort of odd intellectual masturbation and she also has exhibitionist inclinations which if you watched, you might have noticed. She keeps holding my hand whenever we have people around, and every five minutes, in a variety of ways, keeps on repeating how beautiful I am or how I excite her. But as soon as we are left to ourselves, she suddenly alters, her way of behaving with me immediately changes, as if she becomes a completely different person. That's that.

'. . . SO I THOUGHT
I WOULD START A
RELATIONSHIP WITH
A WOMAN WHEN THE
OPPORTUNITY ARISES.'

— *Amrita Sher-Gil*

LETTER 27
MARRIED LOVE
Various to Marie Stopes
1918

Born in 1880 in Edinburgh, Scotland, author and
academic Marie Stopes wrote the controversial and
ground-breaking Married Love (1918), which discussed
birth control, marriage and sex. The book's widespread
condemnation merely made it more popular, with sales
of 2,000 copies recorded its first two weeks. It also
provoked letters from far and wide, of which these are
just two. Three years later, Stopes caused yet more
controversy when she and her husband opened Britain's
first family planning clinic in London, named the
Mothers' Clinic – a space in which women could access
free advice and contraception, unconnected to their
doctor's surgery. Further clinics were soon opened
across the UK and today there are more than 600
Marie Stopes International centres worldwide.

THE LETTERS

Dr Marie Stopes

Dear Madam,

As you refer in your important book "Married
Love" to the question of positions, I think that as
one who has had more than twenty years of
unusually happy married life I may be allowed a
few words of supplement to what you have
written, and you will use your own judgment
as to making any use of them in view of the
reticence which is desirable on this delicate
subject.

I don't think the experience of the lady who
told you she felt almost suffocated each time can
be exceptional. I myself know of an unusually
lovely young wife saying she wished her husband
was not so heavy, and the legal term "feme
covert" for a married woman points to old
custom. Yet it is shocking to think of her delicate
body being strained and pinned down under a
heavy man, and it both foolish and needless. My
bride soon found the right position and it is so
absolutely comfortable for both that we have never

had any other. I lie on my back, she lies upon me with her left leg between mine and my left between hers. Then I turn partly on my right side and we settle cosily into the position evidently intended by nature. The lady is in the position of honour on a sort of throne, and as she can talk as well as move freely there is no risk of her being left nervy and as you say in the air through premature ejaculation. And when all is over both relax without change of position and even without withdrawal into the greatest and most refreshing sleep. A letter such as I understand you to refer to without disapproval is used except when conception is deliberately desired by both. In what you say about coition during pregnancy is your reference to the example of animals quite sufficient as it stands? The male animal resorts freely to other females; may not your words be perverted as pointing men in that direction? If the husband stands by the bedside and the wife lies across it he may get a moderate coition without exciting her, and I don't think she is reluctant. Of course he will use the most extreme tenderness and consideration for her, and not go on too long. I don't think you say anything about the narrow separate beds which have been introduced in England from continental countries. I don't see

how they can allow comfortable positions, but we
have never used them.

yours sincerely

A happy husband and father

* * *

Dr. Stopes
Go back to your own Country and preach your
dirty methods there. Decent English people are
disgusted at your filthy suggestions in "Married
Love." Sexual gratification is not the only thing that
makes life worth living, as you seem to think. At
any rate, yours is a paying game, and naturally that
is what matters most to you.

Go back home.

LETTER 28
IF ONLY
Percy Grainger to Karen Holten
2 October 1910

Australian composer Percy Grainger was just twelve years old when he made his first public performance as a pianist. By the time of his death from cancer in 1961, he was considered one of the great symphony composers in musical history. Ten years after his death, just as he had stipulated when depositing it in 1956, archivists in Melbourne opened a huge box he had spent a long time preparing. In it, they found dozens of homemade whips and other devices used by Grainger and his sexual partners, pieces of clothing, some of them bloodstained, worn during these BDSM sessions, and countless photographs of him and his lovers in action. All of this, and more, now resides in the 'Lust Branch' of the Grainger Museum in Victoria, Australia. Also held there are his letters, of which this is just one. It was written to a Danish music student named Karen Holten, with whom he corresponded for many years. It is difficult to imagine letters more sexually explicit.

THE LETTER

Grand Hotel
Kristiansund N.

2.10.1910

You, little comrade, will so well suit the sea and
rain and primitive pleasures. You have the
Scandinavian woman's toughness and singleness and
contentment with unpleasant extremes.

Someone like you wakens naturalness in
someone like me. I don't only love you with my
English sharp singular sensuality and my personal
cruelty (although I do that as well) but I love you
with international impersonal naturalness, I long
not only to love you as my sensuality demands, I
also long to love you as your sensuality demands,
I want to throw all separators to hell, and glide
gently with my thick strong phallus into your inner
fjords, your smooth oily greasy slimy interior
roads, that fog-up and bewitch away all mental
consciousness, my phallus smelling sharp and
animal-like of rotten fish, your sex passages
smelling sharp and animal-like of something bitter
and sour, and feel the thick rich cream stride
forth from my body's interior dark earth and grow

fruitfully forward against your womanliness's warmth and intoxicating sun, and stride up and forward with maddening thudding pumping pulse, enormous and threatening, till all personality is intoxicated away, till all nationality is sensualised away, till the difference between you and me is only thought and not felt, till I become woman and you become man in our crowning moment, and my life-infecting marrow milk spits forward in your hidden mouth, where my stiff belly-tongue and your love-throat kiss with slimy wet greasy convulsive muscular kisses, tearing and revolutionary, beastly and joyous, and my tight boy's body, solemn, with singing ears and flayed will, pays its full tax of white blood into your Queen's treasure chest, and your soft pliable deluding seducing girl-entrails suck and draw out and consume and digest the stolen contagious world-enrichments, while our 2 forms lie enveloped in a steam of passion, sweaty-smelling under our arms and around our anus, our muscles relax, and grateful tiredness and joyful relief spread over us and our love-wet animal-smelling sexual parts.

Oh, if only you could spit your love-spit into my eyes, if only my mouth could suck your inner woman's penis, if only I could drink your sex-fjord's bitter juice, if only I could bear that you

were sea-sick in my mouth, if only I might bear to
see you eat my 2 testicles like boiled eggs, if only
my 2 eyes were 2 small hairy caves (like your
anus) and your 2 nipples were 2 stiff pointed
finger-thick phalli which you could bore into my
brain, so my life could be extinguished in ecstasy
like an electric lamp.

Percy

PERMISSION CREDITS

Every effort has been made to trace copyright holders and obtain their permission for the use of copyright material. The publisher apologises for any errors or omissions and would be grateful if notified of any corrections that should be incorporated in future reprints or editions of this book.

LETTER 1 Margaret Mead, letter 'An instrument of joy' to her sister, January 11, 1926, from *To Cherish the Life of the World: The Selected Letters of Margaret Mead*, 2006, Basic Books. Reproduced with permission of the American Anthropological Association. Not for sale or further reproduction.

LETTER 2 Patrick Leigh Fermor, letter 'What gloomy tidings about the CRABS' to Enrica Soma, 11 August 1961, from *Dashing for the Post: The Letters of Patrick Leigh Fermor*, John Murray, 2016. Reproduced by permission of John Murray Publishers, an imprint of Hodder and Stoughton Limited.

LETTER 5 Dorothy Day, letter 'If bodies please thee, praise God on occasion of them' to Forster Batterham, December 10, 1932, from *All the Way to Heaven. The Selected Letters of Dorothy Day*, edited by Robert Ellsberg. Marquette University Press, copyright © 2010 Milwaukee, Wisconsin, USA. Used by permission of the publisher. All rights reserved. www.marquette.edu/mupress.

LETTER 8 John Cheever, letter 'This astonishing pilgrimage' from *The Letters of John Cheever*, ed by Benjamin Cheever, copyright © 1988 by Benjamin Cheever. Reproduced with the permission of The Random House Group Limited; and Touchstone, a division of Simon & Schuster, Inc. All rights reserved.

LETTER 9 Dora Carrington, letter 'Do not think I rejoice in being sexless' to Mark Gertler, 16 April 1915, published in *Carrington Letters: Her Art, Her Loves, Her Friendships* by Dora Carrington, Chatto & Windus, copyright © The Estate of Dora Carrington. Reproduced by permission of the author c/o Rogers, Coleridge & White Ltd., 20 Powis Mews, London W11 1JN.

LETTER 10 Anaïs Nin, letter 'Sex does not thrive on monotony', to The Collector, undated, from *The Diary of Anaïs Nin, Volume 3, 1939–1944*, copyright © 1969 by Anais Nin, renewed 1997 by Rupert Pole and Gunther Stuhlmann. Reproduced by permission of Houghton Mifflin Harcourt Publishing Company and the Anaïs Nin Trust. All rights reserved.

LETTER 11 J.M. Coetzee, letter 'Dear Paul' April 24, 2009, from *Here and Now: Letters 2008-2011* by Paul Auster and J. M. Coetzee,

LETTER 25 Martha Gellhorn, letter 'I was the worst bed partner in five continents' to Betsy Drake, 3 September 1972 from *The Letters of Martha Gellhorn*, Chatto & Windus, 2006, by Caroline Moorehead. Reproduced by permission of The Random House Group Limited.

LETTER 28 Percy Grainger, letter 'If Only' to Karen Holten, 2 October 1910, from *Farthest North of Humanness: Letters by Percy Aldridge Grainger*, Palgrave Macmillan, 1985. Reproduced by kind permission of the Estate of George Percy Grainger.

ACKNOWLEDGEMENTS

It requires a dedicated team of incredibly patient people to bring the Letters of Note books to life, and this page serves as a heartfelt thank you to every single one of them, beginning with my wife, Karina – not just for her emotional support during such stressful times, but for the vital role she has played as Permissions Editor on many of the books in this series. Special mention, also, to my excellent editor at Canongate Books, Hannah Knowles, who has somehow managed to stay focused despite the problems I have continued to throw her way.

Equally sincere thanks to all of the following: Teddy Angert and Jake Liebers, whose research skills have helped make these volumes as strong as they are; Rachel Thorne and Sasmita Sinha for their crucial work on the permissions front; the one and only Jamie Byng, whose vision and enthusiasm for this series has proven invaluable; all at Canongate Books, including but not limited to Rafi Romaya, Kate Gibb, Vicki Rutherford and Leila Cruickshank; my dear family at Letters Live: Jamie, Adam Ackland, Benedict Cumberbatch, Aimie Sullivan, Amelia Richards, and Nick Allott; my agent, Caroline Michel, and everyone else at Peters, Fraser & Dunlop; the many illustrators who have worked on the beautiful covers in this series; the talented performers who have lent their stunning voices not just to Letters Live, but also to the Letters of Note audiobooks; Patti Pirooz; every single archivist and librarian in the world; everyone at Unbound; the team at the Wylie Agency for their assistance and understanding; my foreign publishers for their continued support; and, crucially, my family, for putting up with me during this process.

Finally, and most importantly, thank you to all of the letter writers whose words feature in these books.

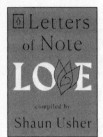

LETTERS OF NOTE: LOVE

Revealing deep, eternal truths from the heart, this intimate collection of letters traces all of love's incarnations, from first blush and mutual enchantment to unrequited feelings and the ache of passions past. It offers a rare, passionate, and timeless look at what it means to love and be loved.

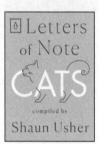

LETTERS OF NOTE: CATS

This utterly charming collection offers a warm and friendly look at the place that cats occupy in our hearts and lives. These letters capture the profound delight of having or observing a cat, and they reveal a keen insight into feline nature as well as our own.

LETTERS OF NOTE: MUSIC

Riffing on their passions and surroundings, the artists and entertainers in this volume candidly reveal the sources of their inspiration, what music means to them, why they create it, and so much more. This rich and engaging collection of letters celebrates the resonance that music, in its many forms and variations, brings to our lives.

PENGUIN BOOKS

 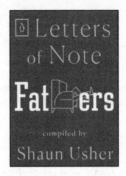 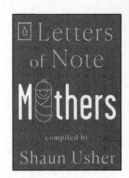